Blessing to you —

Relevant Church

Relevant
Church
A God-given goal

An inspirational journey into
ministry and church life

REVD LES ISAAC

ASCENSION TRUST

You are the salt of the earth.
But if the salt loses its saltiness,
how can it be made salty again?
It is no longer good for anything,
except to be thrown out and trampled by men.

Matthew 5:13

CONTENTS

ACKNOWLEDGEMENTS

My thanks are due in particular to Roger and Faith Forster, Julaine Headman, James Kane, David Perry and the Trustees of Ascension Trust. I am very grateful to Prue Knowles for her careful reading of the typescript.

INTRODUCTION

Since my last book, *Dreadlocks*, many valuable experiences with God have taken me on a journey into church life: church life which majors on community relevance and equipping church members to be salt and light outside the four walls of the church building. Matthew 5:13-16 says,

> You are the salt of the earth, but if the salt loses its saltiness, how can it be made salty again? It is no longer good for anything except to be trampled by man. You are the light of the world. A city on a hill cannot be hidden. Neither do people light a lamp and put it under a bowl. Instead they put it on its stand and it gives light to everyone in the house. In the same way, let your light shine before men that they may see your good deeds and praise your Father in heaven.

I have learnt much from the challenges of pastoral work and evangelistic ministry. I have also developed convictions and a passion for what I believe the Church should be doing, and should aim to become, in its own community. In this book I hope to share with you something of that passion and the practical steps I took to achieve my God-given goal of 'relevant church'.

The Church, I believe, should be a place of training, mentoring and empowerment. Many Christians do want to be involved in sharing the gospel relevantly, but they feel that they are not equipped to do so. They receive good sermons but what they are in greater need of is training and practical support to do the task. Seeing people develop in confidence and in their ability to share Jesus is, for me, a great delight.

The Church should be an asset to the community. Over the years the Church has not always been relevant, but communities are still looking to the Church for answers and help. To be a valuable asset to our community a church must listen to the concerns and needs of local people. I also know that we need to "scratch people where they itch", rather than do what we think might be vaguely helpful. The times I have allowed for investigation and questioning have always yielded results. Knowing where exactly to start and what will be of most value requires waiting on God for his direction and confirmation for the way forward.

The Church should be a catalyst for personal, corporate and community change. It has given me great joy over the years to see members of my local congregation knowing a release in their giftings as they have risen to the challenge to get involved, find their niche, and be all that God wants them to be in the church and to their community.

The Church is not a building, but a community itself. It is made up of people serving other people. Encouraging church members to look beyond their own circumstances and see the greater need outside the church doors, and to instill a desire to serve and love, is often a great challenge. It is a challenge to change mindsets! A fervent prayer team and a humble and willing core leadership team is what God always gives me to set the wheels in motion for change.

This book describes the processes of change I have experienced: change towards being more outward-looking;

change in terms of being less individualistic; changes in our ways of working so that roles become complementary. The more I have desired the way forward, the more I have learnt to listen to God. Out of my listening I have been able to acknowledge gaps in spiritual and practical resources, in leadership and in wider church life. I have become creative and innovative in my approach to situations which are potentially discouraging. I have stepped out into the public arena to seek partnerships with other organisations whose work will complement that of the Church in the community. I wanted to do and be, as part of God's Church on earth, all that God has asked of me.

In all of this there were many uneasy 'white water' rides, but God, who knew my heart's desire to reach out and be relevant and effective, helped and enabled me to achieve much. So this book is about my journey, my passion, and the lessons I have learnt. My hope is that you might be inspired and encouraged to try new things, step over your church threshold and, with your congregation, become 'relevant church'.

One

TRANSITION

The four of us children – Lemina, Vernon, Cynthia and me – arrived at Heathrow airport in March 1965. Four little black faces amid all the white ones. We were looking for our parents, whom we had not seen for four years, since they left us in the care of our grandmother. In fact, I had no idea what they looked like. I knew I would know them when we found them, or they found us, but I couldn't conjure up a mental picture of them.

"So this is England," I thought, blinking my seven-year-old eyes in disbelief at the sea of people around me. I ran, stumbling as I tripped over my untied shoelaces, after my older sister Lemina who, at the grand age of ten, had become our leader. We kept moving, not sure where we were going, but sure that it was best to follow everybody else. Only hours before we had been in the sweltering coconut and sugarcane climate of the West Indies, and England's spring was not welcoming. Only Lemina seemed in any way agitated, feeling obliged to touch each one of us in turn, as if to make sure we were all still there.

Our parents eventually found us huddled together near the customs desks, and interrupted the wandering dream into which I had lapsed as I studied more of the strange white faces around me. My father, Enoch Isaac, seemed big to me. But I suppose it was more that I was so small, because it was stockiness rather than height that gave him an appearance of bulkiness. He looked at me with cold eyes, but just a hint of a smile made me feel secure as he picked me up and gave me a rib-crushing squeeze. My mother, Victoria, was darker skinned than my father, and her very colour made me feel more at home. She was in her twenties, quite a few years younger than my father, and she was well-built and fit-looking. She chuckled and gurgled as she hugged us each in turn, planting a damp kiss on my forehead and repeating my name over and over again.

We were hustled out of the airport and into a waiting car. I spent almost the entire trip staring wide-eyed out of the window, taking in the suburban scenes of London, the giant city that was just getting into the full swing of the sixties. To me, it was the land of milk and honey, subject of so many bedtime stories. Yet the stories hadn't told me of the sprawling bricks and concrete which formed a totally new landscape for me. But here was the ultimate dream being realised. The ambition of every child back home in John Hughes village: to be in England.

Learning to hate

The cramped Islington basement flat where we lived contrasted starkly with the large, rambling house in my village back home, instantly bringing a rush of new fears to me. How could the four of us children, so used to running barefoot from the house to play on the beach, get accustomed to this dark, damp flat? In weeks to come, as the driving rain sent torrents running down the steps and brought ugly green and black damp patches to the walls, I would close my eyes and try to cling to the fading memories of my calypso sunshine island.

I missed the simple way of life, the ramshackle fishing boats, tatty straw hats and the old beggar in my neighbourhood who would shout to me, "Hey, kid, ya got any mangoes, boy?" A big change that I soon noticed was the way I was no longer taking my life in my hands when I met an adult on the street. In Antigua, passing the time of day with your elder was not a rule to be neglected but, to my amazement, nobody in this strange country seemed to talk to one another. I even tried pulling faces at several adults and, to my surprise, I was ignored!

As consciously as a child of my age could, I determined to make the most of this green land of fair-haired strangers, and there and then decided the sheer enormity of the place would not overwhelm me, and that Les Isaac would never be second to anyone. And even then, the seething aggression began to well up in me, even before my first real encounter with racial prejudice and my first bruising from the white boy's fists.

Alfred Pritchard School was a big Victorian building. Roman Catholic downstairs, Church of England upstairs, and attended by an increasing number of black children from the West Indies. As soon as our mother left us for our first day, Vernon and I were being called "golliwogs" by other white children.

"What's a golliwog?" I asked my older brother. I didn't get a response because Vernon didn't know either. We found out one teatime while studying the label on the jar of jam with its crude motif of a black man.

Each day at school brought a new awareness that we were classed as different creatures, and one of the first big words I learned was "prejudice". One day I found myself surrounded by four white boys in the playground. When they snarled at me "Golliwog," I was suddenly aware that this was more than name-calling. One of them came close enough to let a fast right jab fly, my head jerked painfully back, and blood trickled from my nose. That was the moment when I really discovered my temper…and my strength. As the four of them lashed out together, I grabbed the first object that came to hand – a rounders bat. I had time to lay out one of my attackers before a teacher intervened and gripped me by the ear. She held my ear so tightly I screamed out in pain, kicking and struggling. And while she held me, the four attackers spat, punched and kicked at me, and she did nothing to stop them.

I learned fast that I was hated by many because of my skin, and people would take advantage of me whenever they could. I made friends with other West Indian children, and the white boys quickly became less friendly, viewed often as the enemy. And I soon learned how to hate.

In the sixties, black ghettos sprang up all over north London, not to mention Wolverhampton and Bradford. When I was ten my family moved to a large housing estate in Camden where, however, each of us was as conspicuous as if we had sported two heads. We were the first black family to move in. Refusing to be bullied, Vernon and I made friends with most of the kids of our age on the estate. For a short time it was almost as if colour didn't matter anymore. But the dream was shattered on the many occasions when older boys either moved in or passed through, disrupting friendly soccer games and neighbourhood larks with their taunts of "nigger" and "wog".

On one occasion when I had been sent to the shops by my mother, I found the pavement in front of me blocked by four tough-looking white youths. I thought about turning to run and, looking over my shoulder, with a certain amount of relief saw Vernon sprinting to my side. One of the youths took off his belt, and as he swung it around his head he growled, "Come and get it, nigger boys." Vernon took a step forward. The youth hesitated, having expected both of us to make a break for it, and then he swiped at Vernon with the belt. Vernon held out his arm, the belt wrapped itself around it harmlessly, and the weapon was wrenched viciously from the youth's hands. Encouraged by this success, the two of us pitched in, with flying arms and fists, and within seconds the four boys turned and ran.

Naked aggression like this was unexpected, and a growing nightmare. White men to me had always been Americans, and the occasional Englishman back home in Antigua had only been prepared to swing a fist if it meant there would be more rum as a result. I remember a big white American evangelist, with enormous sweat patches under his arms and sweat drops running off his nose as he preached. I could picture in my mind the fat cigar the bulky missionary puffed throughout his sermon, and how I spent much of the time wondering how a man could talk with a thing that size in his mouth.

I could also remember singing, "Blessed assurance, Jesus is mine." The hundred or so people at the open-air meeting that day had sung it at least three times. I had heard the preacher saying something about Jesus loving everybody, and that all people belonged to him. Yet I had a picture of Jesus in my mind, and he was a white man. Could it be that white people with their white Jesus could hate black people and want to hurt them? And why wasn't there a black Jesus to help people like me?

To me, the local church near the estate was a breeding ground for the attitudes that made me a victim. It was a white man's church. Suspicious looks from prim and proper church-goers wearing their Sunday best just made me feel that God wasn't interested in West Indians. And they talked another language that I could not understand, especially the minister in his flowing robes. I went there because of my parents' compulsive sense of religious duty. The whole family had to go every week. The highlight of my week was wrenching off my tie after getting out of church.

Vernon had been a year at Archway Secondary School in the heart of Islington when I changed schools and joined him at the age of eleven. It was a world of bigger white boys with mean hearts, most of them with very different ideas, except in the realm of discrimination. Resplendent in my new blazer, neat tie and smart trousers, I was a prime target for any aggro that was going. The "softy boys" cowered at one end of the playground. The "bad boys" dragged heavily on their cigarettes at the other, noticeable with their heavy boots and turned-up Levi's. I wasn't sure to which end I belonged, but I seemed to be drawn to the mean end. On that very first day I was lured into a fight, in response to the words, "You offerin' me out?", a challenge that I knew meant a meeting after school. Word got around the entire school that there would be a fight involving a new boy, who happened to be a West Indian, and a white bully. As I came out through the main gate at four o'clock I saw a large crowd yelling "knuckle" over and over again.

There were no formalities. I didn't even see the right hook coming, and it split my lip. Fury boiled up in me immediately. I flew at the white boy, fists flailing, and we fell heavily to the ground. Word spread that Les Isaac was tough, a new champ. In the following weeks I got a reputation as one of the best fighters in the school, second only to the unquestioned hard boys who ruled the roost.

Gangs and geezers

I developed a set of close friends, three boys who, like me, were not yet in their teens. We mimicked the skinheads of

our day, and with our hands in our pockets, heavy boots
scuffing the playground tarmac, we spoke with our fellow
"geezers" about how many girlfriends we had. The four of
us, Martin, Kostos, David and myself, frequently stood by
each other in neighbourhood skirmishes. We didn't think
much of attending classes at school, and although we
generally signed on at the morning registration, whether we
appeared at the lunch time registration was determined by
how much fun we were having about town.

Sometimes Lemina would write me a fabricated
note excusing me from school, for my mother was always
too busy at work to keep tabs on us children. A regular
morning jaunt was to Regent's Park and London Zoo.
Lunch was invariably at a café with enough pinball
machines to keep the four of us happy. And afternoons
were usually spent at the cinema. We had found a way to
open fire exits from the outside, so we could avoid using
the front entrance. This would last for a week or two at a
time. Then we would have a period at school, just to make
sure our faces were seen.

One day the four of us, having arranged our usual
bunk from school, headed for Kostos's home. It was a
comfortable house by the local standards, pleasantly large
and very well furnished. Kostos's parents both worked, so
the house was empty. We made ourselves at home, lighting
cigarettes as we lounged in easy chairs. Kostos would often
open up the drinks cabinet to admire its contents, and I
would drink generous measures of whisky from expensive
glasses.

We talked about possible sources for cash because
we were always broke. On one occasion the conversation
came round to the fact that there had to be some cash in
Kostos's house, or a supply which would not be missed by

a successful businessman like Kostos's father. That line of thought led us to the gas and electricity meters. It was while forcing these open that we found a new method of securing a regular income: every telephone box in the district contained a cash box waiting to be raided.

I grew accustomed to walking around with my right hand permanently in my jacket pocket, fingering the lethal flick knife I had taken to carrying. It nearly landed me in court, for although I had a masterful knack of avoiding justice at crucial moments, I came close to throwing away my freedom on numerous occasions.

I remember one escape from the clutches of the law, which was frankly inexplicable. During a school outing to an art gallery, my authority was challenged by a tall, tough-looking boy, who looked me in the eye and said quietly, "I'm not afraid of you, rastus." That word made something snap inside me. My eyes flashed, and my right hand flew from my pocket, with a flash of silver. If the teacher hadn't forced his way between us, I might have dangerously wounded the youth. As it was, I inflicted two superficial cuts, although serious enough to merit long discussions by senior school staff about the possibility of calling in the police.

Was I lucky? My classmates said so. Or would it have been better for a magistrate to have attempted to stop my reckless life going on in its downward direction? If that had happened, the terrifying violence that was to etch deep emotions into my life might not have occurred, but neither would the deep spiritual reaction that ultimately resulted.

In response to a beating that I and a friend named Bernie took at a club in Islington, I became involved in rabble-rousing, the purpose of which was revenge. We announced to about two hundred recruited lads that there was to be a crew fight against skinheads from the Finchley area. The small army that gathered at Archway was full of pent-up frustration. Only a handful of us were actually looking for revenge; in the rest there was a mixture of resistance to parents, society and police that was waiting for release.

The fight was vicious. Youths were stabbed, children beaten, and blood ran in the streets. The battle raged for only ten minutes before the police arrived, but it was long enough for the youths to do a lot of damage to each other. There were a number of arrests. The papers the next day were full of news of riots and gang warfare. And I was battle-hardened at the tender age of thirteen.

Beneath the party spirit

At about this time in my bloodthirsty career I started to turn more and more to the youth clubs that had sprung up in my area. Putting the boot in was not such good fun without other things in life to give the spice of variety, and there were pretty girls in these clubs. The aggro was limited in these clubs, as dancing and table tennis drained the energy otherwise used for fighting.

'Blues' were all-night West Indian parties that started at eleven in the evening and went right through to seven the next morning. Three or four rooms would be set aside in a terraced house, and you would pay an entrance fee on the door. Loud music flowed non-stop and the atmosphere was hazy and heavy. Food and cans of beer were on sale. The rooms were jammed solid with West Indians aged from twelve to fifty, wearing large floppy tams, berets or woolly hats, adorned in expensive Crombies, smart American brogues, flashy silk handkerchiefs – all the gear that epitomised the black London resurgence of unique identity. Some wore the new-style dreadlocks – long but thin curls distinct to the new Rastafarian cult which was growing so rapidly in Britain at that time.

At some Blues the records were more frequently of Rastamen, and ganja (marijuana) was passed around more openly. It all started to get a hold on me, gripping my imagination as a whole new way of socialising unfurled before me. Instead of the bluntly physical communion of violence, here was the challenge of a spiritual fellowship with my own kind.

I liked Blues. I liked buying my fifty pence worth of ganja neatly folded in a piece of newspaper, and I liked rolling a 'spliff' for a pleasant evening's smoke. I enjoyed the sensation of being at peace with my surroundings as I floated into 'highs', and the marked contrast to the heady days of street fighting made it all the more of an adventure. Coupled with this new habit, I began to let my appearance slip. Gone was the smart dress code of the skinhead, and my closely cropped hair was now allowed to grow at random without the discipline of regular combing.

I started to take ganja to school. There, my close circle of friends and I would smoke pot during breaks, and even on rare occasions, took the risk of smoking it in the class when the teacher was otherwise distracted, although only if there was an open window nearby to waft away the smell. In my usual crafty fashion, I managed to avoid being caught with the illegal drug, although I did run into trouble when I was caught with cigarettes. I didn't realise it, but I was allowing myself to walk headlong into a carefully laid trap that was designed to ensnare my life – anybody's life – and never let go.

Looking from black face to black face, I saw sadness behind the party spirit. These were my brothers, my people. But where did we all come from, and what were our roots? Why had my ancestors been exploited so much and with such cruelty? What right had white men to do such horrible things to my people? And even through the haze of pot smoke, I knew the new friends I had made found it in themselves to be angry, and that anger welled up in me also.

African hero

My new friends talked of Jah and Ras Tafari, and it sparked off something inside me. Ras Tafari (the ending pronounced 'eye') was Haile Selassie, emperor of Ethiopia, and heralded as the saviour of black people. More and more he filled my mind as I felt as if I was simultaneously searching and finding. One of the many songs that were being sung about Ras Tafari and the ideas associated with him particularly caught my imagination. It went,

> Freedom, O freedom
> O freedom over me,
> Before I be a slave,
> I'll skip over my grave,
> And I'll go home
> To my father and to be free.

I wanted identity. I wanted someone I could relate to, and I wanted spiritual reality. I felt trapped, and needed peace inside and freedom from the things that nagged remorselessly at my conscience. I was so attracted to this

Rastaman, and he seemed to offer the only road to the inner utopia that now gripped my thoughts.

I determined to know more about Rastafarians, and eagerly devoured their philosophical answers to my incessant questions. With this new direction, I stopped my aggressive involvement in the youth scene of those days and embarked on a new, peaceful, approach to life. I turned my thoughts to Africa, and even decided that I wanted to go to the continent where my ancestral roots were. When I looked around me and saw the treatment handed out to my black brothers and sisters, the police harassment and ignorant discrimination, I began to wonder why my parents had brought me to this land where I had to make a go of my life. But I knew that somehow Jah (God) would help me overcome these problems, and the great mystical being would help me get to Africa one day.

I also noticed that my own people were divided. They were frequently malicious towards one another and their priorities seemed all wrong. The black brotherhood needed to sort itself out. Many West Indian girls were having several children before they even reached adulthood, and that appalled me. West Indians called themselves brothers and sisters, but still the men were abusing their young women and not showing them love and respect. The men and youths fought with each other, using fearful weapons. They even killed one another.

I spent many evenings in deep discussion with my new friends around an open Bible, talking about the black man, about Africa, and West Indians. We talked about going to Africa. We talked about God and how he created black men. We smoked ganja in a communal pipe that was passed around like the Red Indian's peace pipe. All night long we delved deeper into what we thought was the truth to set us free. On Sundays the hazy discussions would start in the early afternoon, centering on Jah and our 'Jesus', Haile Selassie. The Jesus of the Christians was a white man's saviour, but Jah had raised up a new 'Jesus' for black men.

Rasta life

Rastafarianism is much more than a set of religious beliefs. It offers answers to the complex problems faced by black people, and gives a resilience in the face of oppressive poverty and the dire struggle of everyday living. The phrases that Ras Tafari used when he was crowned emperor gave rise to the doctrine of the divinity of Selassie. He claimed to be a direct descendant of King David, and therefore the scripture in Revelation, 'See, the Lion of the tribe of Judah, the root of David, has triumphed' (Revelation 5:5), became the basis of teaching that Selassie was a redeemer for Rastas. After his coronation, the acceptance of Selassie as the living God increased and, simultaneously, there was a frantic search of the Scriptures for a basis for this. Any passage of the Bible sufficed if it lent weight to the doctrine, but the main ones used were Isaiah 43:1-5 and 24-28, Ezekiel 37:19-25 and Revelation 1:14 and 17-18.

Race is a big issue for Rastas, and it is particularly expressed in the certainty of the coming ruin of 'Babylon', believed to be white society and its allies. To the Rasta, whites are the oppressors and the allies of Satan. Blacks, on the other hand, are seen as God's chosen people, although this does not mean that all black people are included in the special race. Those who help white society in any way are 'lost sinners'.

Rastas have a hope, in both a spiritual and a physical sense, of a return to Africa. The spiritual aspect of this is the regaining of the dignity of their forefathers which was robbed when they were enslaved. They are searching for the reality of who they are and where they are going. Most Rastas believe they are reversing the process that took place with slavery by their diet, dress, hairstyle, speech, political and spiritual beliefs. But they are also looking to return physically to Africa, not just to African ways. There is a parallel here with the Christian expectation of heaven and eternal life.

Rastafarianism states that the spirit of Ras Tafari is universal and eternal, thus getting round the problem of his death in 1975. For me however, it was in life that Selassie began to lose his divinity.

One evening I was at a friend's house to watch a television programme in which my new hero was scheduled to make an appearance. Haile Selassie was to talk about the Ethiopian civil war. I remember how excited and full of eager anticipation I was. As I watched the screen, the great man climbed out of a huge, shining limousine, casting coins to the impoverished crowds of Addis Ababa. His regal attitude belied his small stature, yet he seemed so far removed from his subjects and was only concerned with a token gesture of compassion. It was at this moment that my faith in this man began to crumble. On the very first occasion I set eyes on Haile Selassie, I knew this man was a mere mortal and not 'God', for if he was divine, surely he could do something more for his suffering people? But I still I searched in the Rastafarian way for answers.

The search

Not long after that television broadcast, I met Zac, a man with whom I found a strange mutual trust. The tall and thin West Indian spoke freely of Jesus and his miraculous provision for Zac's family, and how it was possible for a man to actually have a meaningful relationship with God. Zac would stuff endless tracts peddling his brand of Christianity into my pockets. One day I pulled out one of these leaflets and read it while I was at my sister's house. It was a small event that prompted a prophetic remark by Lemina, who thought I was merely skipping from one fad to another.

"You goin' to be a preacher man now?" she goaded me.

"No," I replied, "but a man has to look into these things because these are the words of the Almighty." The Almighty, who had had his hand on my life ever since it began seventeen years earlier, at last found the kind of response he had looked for in me for so long.

The words I read in that tract bored deep into my mind and heart. They puzzled me. Somehow I felt as if I was groping for something that I could not fully understand, so I read and re-read the message contained in the pamphlet. I was being driven by a force that raised many questions in me, and the desire to talk and reason with other people on similar spiritual quests. The conversations would wind on and on, sometimes going somewhere, sometimes doubling back.

Then I met a girl called Lily at a fun fair in West Hampstead and found that my searching for God was even affecting my relationships with women. As I chatted her up it transpired that she was the sister of a black youth called Davison who had clearly 'got religion'. Indeed, Davison had earned himself quite a reputation by shouting out "Hallelujah" at the top of his voice in various public places, and was generally thought to be crazy. But if his behaviour was the result of a genuine spiritual experience, I wanted to find out about it.

I asked Lily about her brother's conversion.

"Oh he jus' come home one day an' announced he was followin' dis Jesus," she said. So I asked her if she had any experience of God. She hadn't, although she said she thought she believed in him. And all of a sudden I lost interest in this pretty girl, because I wanted to find a greater reality, and she seemed unable to shed any light on the pathway which I was exploring. When I eventually got to know Davison himself, I realised that this was a man who had peace and joy, even if he did act a bit strange from time to time.

But now God was more important to me than people, and certainly more important than casual relationships. Even as a teenager I had found the Rastafarian ideal of having a number of women to sleep with and call my own a satisfying way of life. But now I was searching for God, and God was more important than women. It was like sitting at a table with a sumptuous feast and losing your appetite.

Mother and father

After leaving school in 1973 at the age of sixteen I became an apprentice plumber. At this time, when I was at the height of my search for God, I was living at my mother's home and giving her a cut of my £11 take-home pay. My parents had been divorced for some time and my mother looked after all four of us children. However, I would often disappear for days, sleeping at the home of one of my women, and return unannounced. My mother didn't worry about that.

But in 1974 she was taken ill. When I returned from a five-day absence, my brother Vernon told me that she had become ill and the doctor had been called. She looked drawn and frail, appearing much older than her thirty-eight years, and I took her immediately to hospital. There I sat with her for hours, and once, near the end, she caught my eye with renewed awareness and her look said, "How will they cope without me?" I felt cold and suddenly alone.

The next morning I had to attend a college plumbing course. Half-way through a lecture the door opened and a member of staff at the college poked his head around the door and called out my name. My heart started to beat rapidly. My legs went weak. I had to cough and splutter before I could speak to identify myself. I knew by the look on the man's face what he was going to say. He confirmed that my mother had died. I left the college in a daze. I didn't know what I was doing or where I was going, I just walked like an automaton. When I found the rest of my family, they were in the same state.

Three days later I saw my mother's body in the coffin, and for the first time in my life the full reality of death dawned upon me. As a youth I had several times handled a weapon not caring if it took another's life, but I did not know what death was really like. I had seen people die by pretence in the cinema, and had equated the death of people on news reports as the same fake thing. Now death had taken my mother.

From that moment I found myself pleading with the mystical figure of Selassie to intervene. I started to smoke more ganja than could possibly be good for me, and my conversation was continually of Rastafarianism. Morning and evening I drowned my feelings of grief in marijuana and Ras Tafari.

By the time my mother was buried, my father had returned home. His arrival brought new tensions to the Isaac household, particularly between me and him. He was a man of authority, not used to anyone questioning him. What he said went – and that was an explosive thing for me to encounter. It was as if my father intended to carry on in the same way he had when I had been a youngster who needed a good dressing-down from time to time. Dad was a threat, and he frequently squared up to Vernon and me.

The main bone of contention was the way I would stay away from home without announcing my plans and then re-appear on the doorstep a few days later. When my father issued an ultimatum about this behaviour, something snapped inside me. I stepped past my father, went to my room and packed a few things into a small bag, and left the house. When I returned a few days later with the threat still in my mind, I was ready to actually fight with my father. This time it came to nothing, but it wasn't long before we faced each other out again. The conflict continued day in and day out, until finally the question was put: how can there be more than one captain on a ship?

Vernon, as the older brother, calmly told my father that he should leave. But he didn't go, and the friction got worse. My new ethics discarded, I searched high and low for the old machete my mother had owned, intending after much provocation to bring my father to submission. I couldn't find it and determined to get a new one from the army surplus store the next day. Fortunately I was unable to get away from work during my lunch break that day, for my anger had not subsided and I would gladly have bought and used the lethal weapon.

Later that evening on my way home, I passed the restaurant where my cousin George worked as a chef. I wanted to see how he was and as it was only minutes until he finished work, I went into the open mission hall next door to wait. There, sitting in a corner sipping a cup of tea, was a skinny Nigerian looking for someone to talk to. Amos the preacher was the type of Christian who does not believe in luck or chance. So when I, an angry looking youth stepped inside, he was ready to preach. And the way he put the story of Jesus made it almost appear on a screen before my eyes. I could see Calvary, I could see the soldiers, I could hear the smack of hammer on nail and the cry of agony as the huge wooden cross thudded home into its slot and Jesus was left to die.

I never went to the army surplus store. I didn't buy a machete, and I didn't slice open my father's skull. Instead I talked with God.

Two

A NEW SONG

It was God who spoke first. The vivid description Amos
had given me had created an atmosphere in which I just
seemed to be able to commune with the One for whom I
had been searching for so long. A voice in my mind said,
"Les, Rasta is not the way; Selassie is not the way. I am the
way. And I am the truth, and the life as well. Les, depart
from your sin."

During the half-hour walk home I knew I had been
talking to Someone. And during that walk I decided I
wanted to become a Christian. I wanted to know God. At
that moment an awe-inspiring fear came upon me, a fear
of judgement, a fear that if I were to die or this Jesus were
to come back there and then, I would have no excuses and
I would be lost. What could I say to the Son of God? I
then had one of those experiences normally reserved for
those facing death: I saw in an instant my whole life spread
before me and it didn't look very good.

When I arrived home, without a machete and in a
totally different mood, I announced to my family that I
was going to become a Christian. They all ignored me and
when I spoke, Lemina asked me to keep quiet as they were
watching a television programme. I went to my room, and
although I was unable to sleep for thinking about God, I
stayed there all night. I thought about the death of Jesus as
described by Amos, the man from the mission, and I
thought about the possible return of Christ when I wasn't
ready for it. I decided that after work the next day I would
go straight to Amos and talk some more with him.

However, I couldn't find him that day, and so the
final piece of the jigsaw that I knew would give me peace
of mind, eluded me. I couldn't sleep for several nights. I
became bleary-eyed and sluggish at work. I felt as though
my life was full of poison that needed to be removed, but I

didn't know how to go about it and I didn't know how to pray. Many times I fell down by my bed and tried to pray, but I only felt dumb. I felt I had been dumb all my life, and now when I needed words to speak they just wouldn't come. Instead tears came to my eyes. I felt guilty and so dirty before the Almighty God whose presence I could now feel in the room. The stronger the presence of God became, the fouler and dirtier I felt. All my sin was before me, and I knew it to be offensive to this holy Being.

I again struggled to speak. I thought the Lord's prayer might be appropriate, for people in films always seemed to say the Lord's prayer when they needed help. I opened my mouth again and forced myself to speak. But all that came out, with deep sobs, was, "Jesus, you know I don't believe in you, but if you are real, I want you to save me."

After what seemed like an age, I got off my knees, and stood in front of my full-length wardrobe mirror. I stood staring at my reflection for some time, and then I felt as if I was looking through the mirror at something in the wardrobe. My eyes were piercing the glass and the wood and I was looking at a small package in the pocket of one of my jackets. It was ganja. I opened the wardrobe and pulled out the weed which was wrapped in a small piece of newspaper. I opened the window and threw it out with the words, "I don't need you no more."

Immediately a voice said, "Les, you crazy or something?"

But I renewed my vow. "I don't need this no more." I looked in the mirror again. I saw my rasta locks, long and thick; they had not seen a comb for years. I said to myself, "Now you need to let people know you are a child of God, and you don't need locks for that." Within a few days I had my hair cut, and my own glory was removed to make way for the inner glory that God had brought. At last my family took notice of me. My friends in the clubs also took notice of me, for they thought I was slightly mad to refuse their offers of ganja. My talk of going to church was surely just a passing phase, wasn't it? That's what they thought.

New life

I hunted for Amos and brought tears of joy to the little Nigerian's face when I told him what had happened. We spent many hours together, an older, experienced Christian encouraging a spiritual new-born and showing me the ways of God. I remember Amos telling me that I was a new person now, and the world would look different to me, and people would seem different to me. He warned me that friends and family might even turn against me because I would be a threat to them now. I decided it couldn't be true of my friends, but in the coming months I did meet with many obstacles and discouragements in this respect.

In my work situation I soon found out what direct opposition was like. I told my workmates that Jesus loved them, but they didn't want to know. They were shocked and threatened by what I told them, and they covered it up by laughing at me. I was indignant. I reverted to the only way I knew and got aggressive, matching their ridicule with threats, as if using my natural strength would somehow get them to see the truth that Jesus changes lives.

I frequently met old friends in the West End. They all wanted to know where I had been and why I hadn't been to any of my old haunts. I told them all, with my usual enthusiasm, about the change in my life now that I was a Christian. I wanted them to know this good news and how it would give them something to live for.

There were some occasions when I felt a warm glow deep inside when I was speaking of Jesus to people. I knew then that a greater Being had been speaking through me. True, my words may have had a measure of immaturity and a lack of tact about them, but it had been God who stirred me and God who had used me to put the most important message of life across.

Yet the situation in my workplace made me go home each day deeply discouraged. What had I expected? Only that all my friends at work would be falling over themselves to be converted, instantly realising that I was right and that everyone needed a saviour, and should turn to Jesus. But it just didn't happen like that, and my dream was shattered. In my walks back home I once again felt the sense of being trapped in the gloominess of the area.

I prayed, "Lord, why do they not want you? Why do they laugh? Why do they not listen?" Gently and with deep love for this fragile child of his, God showed me how his own Son had been horribly and cruelly rejected. How Jesus had brought people healing and life yet had been spat upon, scorned, betrayed and crucified for all the world to see. The Christian life was not a series of happy events with everything clicking marvellously into place. It was a war: not between religious ideals and the traditions of men, but a struggle between spiritual powers. The ultimate triumph and victory had been won there at that point of humiliation, agony and death, at Calvary.

God's victory was the height of rejection. Now I saw that although I was feeling sorry for myself because my friends had rejected me, this was the place and time to love those who laughed, and to pray earnestly for those who scoffed. For Jesus, who was the enemy of no one but hated by many, said my new way was to love my enemies.

Amos took me to a church in Kennington, south London. It seemed to me that the people there had a power, a driving force that was not to be found in most people. It was an energy that enabled them to lead successful lives in a miserable world. They enjoyed living, while people all around moaned and whined about paltry things like the weather and taxes. They could sing and praise God with great gusto. They could clap and dance just because God was with them. They could pray for great things, even impossible things, as if the strangest result would be that the thing they asked for *didn't* happen.

On one of my early visits to this church, I recall arriving late just as the first hymn was ending: "Floods of joy o'er my soul, like the sea billows roll, since Jesus came into my heart", they sang. The people held out the last note on the word, 'heart', as if wanting to savour the truth of the statement they had just sung, and as it ended there was an eruption of joyful praise, with "Hallelujah" and "I love you Lord" shouted freely from the excited hearts. My own heart beat faster, and I joined in, feeling the adrenalin begin to flow as if I was running out onto a soccer pitch.

This was food and drink to me now. I knew it was because the One these people were singing and talking about was real, and he was there, present in that very building and communing with his people. It was real, but at the same time almost unreal. Different. Like nothing I had ever experienced before. Here there was no doubt that Jesus was Lord, and the most powerful Being in the whole of creation. Yet this great, awesome Being had time for me, a black seventeen-year-old, guilty of many secret and open crimes, a social outcast. Through Jesus I was now at peace with God and actually talking and listening to him. The sheer impact of it made me sit down in my seat while everyone else carried on singing, "This is my story, this is my song, praising my saviour all the day long..." It summed up the most remarkable days in my life. I had a new story, and a new song. It was about my saviour, a man called Jesus who was the Son of God.

Revelation

During one of my customary sessions reading the Bible, I found the words in Zechariah that said, 'Not by might, nor by power, but by my Spirit, says the Lord' (Zechariah 4:6), and I at last understood how a person comes to see and understand God for himself. Who had picked me up by my lapels to make me into a Christian? No one. God had gently and patiently revealed Christ to me by the working of his own Holy Spirit in the circumstances of life. So now I realised that forcing God on people would do no good at all, and in fact could only do harm. The revelation made me feel rather stupid.

On many occasions I prayed that God would help me speak to people; to speak with his words and to love them like he did. As I prayed I had a growing feeling of certainty that as I talked to people about Jesus, God would save them. I just knew that this was how it would be.

I would deliberately go to parties where I knew there would be people I could talk to, and even when the party was in full swing I would find myself in another room with a small group of partygoers debating and reasoning about Jesus. I felt that that was where Jesus was. In my early twenties, in the months and years following my conversion to Christianity, I had to deal with many reactions to my new faith. The questions came thick and fast, and it seemed that my old friends, many of whom struggled to recognise me with my locks cut off, were more interested in compiling a list of the things I didn't do anymore rather than what I now did do.

Many were stunned by the changes in me, and when I went to my old haunts, to pubs, snooker halls and parties, I talked to them for hours about how Jesus was really alive and how he was interested in them. I told them how Jesus accepted and loved them. I prayed fervently for my old friends, and knew that although we were no longer close in the way that we had been, I now had a higher purpose which was to introduce them to Christ.

I was very aware of God calling me to live a holy and righteous life. I knew I needed to be separated from my old self and give my life totally to God. Could I really live out this calling? I held firmly to the scripture, 'Yet to all who received him, to those who believed in his name, he gave the right to become children of God' (John 1:12). At the heart of this challenge, for me, was the need to forgive people the way Jesus forgave and to love people the way he loved.

Davison, infamous for his loud declarations of praise for God, whose faith had been of such interest to me as I chatted-up his sister Lily, became my firm friend at this time. We met at a West Indian church in Haringey and continued to see a lot of each other as his church was running a series of special meetings to which I went, aimed at making a real impact on the godlessness of the area.

One of the distinguishing marks of the new life in Christ which I had come into was my sense of expectancy about every day, and with this came a fresh view of life, my family, my friends, or people I passed on the street. I had begun a new job as a dark-room technician, and as an excitable eighteen-year-old, I had passing dreams of adventure as a photographer on Fleet Street. However, my job took second place to my new found mission of reaching other people for the Lord Jesus Christ.

Davison introduced me to Mike, another young man in whom there was an uncontrollable fire motivating him to tell the world about Jesus. These two friends began to take me under their wing, becoming my mentors. I also searched out my old friend, Zac, one of the first Christians who had made an impact on me. There were several people who spoke words of wisdom and guidance to me in these early days of my new life as a Christian, and I easily fell into the position of shadowing them and being responsive to their spiritual maturity.

I spent a lot of time in prayer and fasting, and enjoyed spending time with people who could provoke me and stir me into sharing my faith. I was, happily, single-minded about Jesus. He had radically changed my life, and I knew God was real. Instinctively I knew that many people's view of God was just the opposite – they believed God to be remote. I carried with me the belief that many people's understanding of God had been warped, and set myself the task of changing that perception wherever and whenever I could.

Film roadshow

One day as Davison, Mike and I were queuing in traffic in my battered Ford Cortina, we watched a long line of people waiting to go into a cinema. As we scanned the faces of the couples and families, Mike said, "Those people need Jesus." Davison and I agreed and, as if a light was dawning over him, Mike continued, "Hey, why don't we get a projector and find somewhere to show Christian films?"

The suggestion brought a positive response. We firmly believed that God was leading us to set up a film-showing enterprise, and although we knew that we would need money to get it off the ground, the Lord would provide everything we needed. We agreed between ourselves that we would make any sacrifice in this cause. Through prayer we received a projector and other vital equipment.

The film roadshow was fully booked in no time. We presented the films wherever we were asked to go, in churches, schools, youth clubs, or in people's homes. We discovered that people were very enthusiastic about watching a film, more so than listening to a preacher. I found that my desire to reach people with the word of God was increased again.

Eventually, Davison and I, along with some other friends, produced a monthly newsletter full of testimony to the work of Jesus Christ, which we named *Lifeline*, and distributed in our neighbourhoods.

Everywhere I encountered people who were hungry for God, and many times God was gracious in opening avenues of communication where there was real racial tension or where conflict was a way of life, or in situations where I was received with aggression and hostility.

As the film ministry grew we were given great opportunities for uniting churches in mission, and the Christian community became excited at the prospect of working together and reaching the locality for the Lord.

In the beginning

I believe that my evangelistic ministry and my mission to reach people with the good news of Jesus was born out of the fact that I simply felt at home on the streets, in pubs and clubs, snooker halls and the like. I was amazed that people wanted to talk about Jesus – and I sensed overwhelmingly that non-Christians were excited and gratified by the opportunity to meet 'real' Christians, and be listened to by them. The people I was meeting were full of their disappointments about the Church as well as their expectations of it. They wanted to talk to Christians who would meet them on their own ground to reason and debate about the gospel.

Together with Mike and Davison, I was invited to more and more places to hold evangelistic meetings, and I felt certain that I was right in the middle of God's plan for London. My hope was to be a catalyst for other Christians and their churches. I wanted, through the work of the Holy Spirit in me, to get to a place where I could encourage, train and develop other Christians in evangelism. I was not critical of the Church, but optimistic. "If people can see me sharing my faith," I thought, "it will help others to do the same." I wanted to stir up as many churches as possible to move into evangelism.

Many times I prayed and fasted over some thorny questions which seemed to be the hard kernel of my young faith, and would not go away: "Why was I called to become a Christian?" and "What is my purpose on earth?" After many months of prayerful analysis, I resolved that my mission on earth was to share God's love and grace purposefully and practically. I have always known that I am called to be relevant and practical when I preach the gospel because I am following Jesus Christ whose saving love was holistic. Through the redemptive work of the cross God meets us whatever condition we are in.

I wanted to demonstrate the gospel in that practical way by making sure it was expressed right where people were. Therefore, I said, "If you are a drug user, then the message of Jesus for you is bound up with how Jesus can help you out of your addiction." Or, "If you are a gunman, the gospel begins for you with getting the gun out of your hands." The message of Jesus has to have a tangible outworking; it has to be contextualised.

All of me

In 1984 I began to formulate plans to work full-time as an evangelist. For my wife, Louise, full-time ministry would have major implications, as we had just bought a house and begun to decorate it, and we were thinking about starting a family. Although she was working herself, I naturally asked myself how I would fulfill my responsibilities as a husband and provide for Louise and a family.

At this point I was working full-time as a training officer at a transport company and fitting as many engagements as I could into the evenings and weekends – showing films with Mike and Davison, speaking at church meetings, talking to people in clubs or on the streets. I also worked in partnership at this time with Andrew Brandon, a local G.P. With Andrew I was involved in leading a large event in Tottenham called the "Christ is the Answer" mission, organised by a group of local churches.

The mission was to run for three weeks, and I had agreed with my manager, Tom, to take two weeks off work. I had asked for the third week too, but as accommodating as he was, he had said that it just wasn't possible. They needed me back at work. The first two weeks Andrew and I spent rushing from one venue to another. We held meetings in doctors' surgeries in the mornings, visited people in the afternoon, preached every evening, hosted lunch clubs and generally shared our faith at every opportunity. In the third week, I went to work during the day, came home, had something to eat, and went straight out to rejoin the mission.

It was at this point that I said to myself that by this time next year, I would like to be in full-time Christian work. It wasn't that it was too tiring to stay in paid employment and work for the Lord; it wasn't that I disliked my job or resented having to work to pay the bills. However, it did matter to me that other staff at the company were beginning to think that I got preferential treatment. Although I was a popular guy at work and everyone knew I was a Christian, even the managers were aware that I would leave one day soon, and I felt it was not an ideal situation. Everyone knew that my Christianity went way beyond the Sunday morning variety.

Simply, my heart wasn't in the work any more, and I wasn't the sort of person to do things by halves. I missed the prayer time and the sharing with people which had filled my days during the "Christ is the Answer" mission.

Tom had been a sympathetic boss to me, and in the course of my work he had often been flexible enough to allow me time off to devote my energies to missions and other events in London. My determination to spend as much time as possible in Christian work, and Tom's realisation (even though he wasn't a believer), that I was truly sold out to God, had led us to an arrangement whereby I took one week off work every month in order to spend time sharing my faith and fulfilling my speaking engagements.

When I delivered my resignation to Tom in the office a few months after the mission in Tottenham, his response reflected many of the thoughts that had passed through my mind.

"But Les," he said bewildered, "it was only a year ago that I signed a mortgage reference form for you. How are you going to pay the mortgage?" I too had questioned how I would support myself as I knew the church I belonged to would not be able to help support me.

He was not totally reassured by my reply. "Look, Tom, a natural man cannot understand the things of the Spirit," I said with all the vigour and passion of a young believer caught up with God.

"This may sound unlikely to you, Tom, but God is going to supply my needs." I remember the look of disbelief on his face, but he went on to offer me the chance of coming back to work for the company on a casual basis whenever I needed to. It was an opportunity I made use of at times when I had fewer speaking engagements than usual, and I was grateful to God for reassuring me in this way and confirming the way forward.

I was confident that God would continue to provide for me. One such gift came through a friend of Louise's with whom she had studied at college. He had since moved to Dover but had heard that I had given up my job and that I would be going to London Bible College for a year. He wrote to us, sending a sizeable cheque, saying that he had received an unexpected tax rebate! Encouragements like this really made me sure that God was in my decision to be full-time in Christian work.

I also had confidence in my wife. She was a person of detail and I relied on her wisdom and foresight. It is difficult to know whether I was naïve in some ways as I contemplated this decision, but I certainly was full of zeal and love for the Lord. I constantly saw the need for the love of Christ in the world, and asked myself, "Who is going to go into the nightclubs, schools and prisons?" My overriding thought was that I needed to make a stand for Jesus, and that motivated me tremendously.

Accepting God's call

After leaving my paid job in October 1985, I embarked on this ministry with all of my time and resources. I enrolled at London Bible College, knowing that it was right at this important juncture in my life to put in place a theological foundation and training. As a probationer in college I was part of the leadership team in my church and, together with the pastor, David Perry, I visited members of the congregation, led meetings and did some preaching on Sunday mornings.

David encouraged and challenged me about my ministry, and although I didn't ultimately envisage myself working within the Church, David helped me to see that there would be a weakness in my ability to work effectively with church leaders if I did not get some experience of pastoral ministry myself. I needed to understand the many complexities of leadership and the nuances of the relationship between church leaders and congregations. At this time, churches did not have room for leaders *without* a pastoral ministry, and I felt that the Lord was confirming this direction for me.

However, I was to discover that this was to be a time of hard training and discipline. Following my probationary year at Bible College, I was asked to take responsibility for the church I was attending in south London, in the capacity of leading elder, following the departure of pastor David Perry to a mission in Brazil. Though I had been used to visiting people alongside David and had been a housegroup leader for some time, it was a great surprise to me to find that the other elders believed there was a call of God upon my life to lead this church. They were men of integrity, I reminded myself, and they had seen something in me which I had yet to see in myself.

Yet my heart had never been alive to working inside a church. The vision I had of myself as a preacher was always in some nightclub or on the streets, not facing a row of pews. However, I accepted the discernment of the leadership of this church, and with it, I accepted God's plans for me through this. That was good enough for me, even though I had not fully worked it out in my own mind.

Three

SHEPHERD

When I looked at the Church in the UK, I saw an introverted institution, an organisation that was holding the fort until Christ came again. Its activities were aimed at those already inside it, and there was a massive gulf between those that were Christians inside the Church and those that were non-Christians outside it. I wanted to spend the majority of my time outside the four walls of the Church.

My vision was to see the gospel shared in places that the Church as a whole was not touching, or where it was not effective. I could see the need for Christians to get into places where there were social problems, violence and crime. I wanted to make my Christianity fit right into that, to go into those areas of life and bring Jesus into them.

In the 1970s, evangelism wasn't on the Church's heart as it is today. The Church was lacking evangelists, and I believed, and still do, that if the Church hasn't got evangelists it will not have a strong evangelistic programme. When the Church has got evangelists it will begin to get a heart, a mind, a strategy for outreach. Evangelism, far from just being one person's gift, is actually the key to challenging and reviving the Church.

When I became a Christian, I soon realised that the more I spoke to people about Jesus, the more I knew I had to get right before God in every area of my life. Evangelism challenges people to live right. In the light of my experience, and that of many Christians, a natural question might be, "Why do we have 'Church'? What lifts today's Church out of the melting pot of emotions and wilfulness which you find in any club or meeting place?"

The early church of the New Testament was not free from problems, far from it. Yet the Bible clearly shows us that it is good for Christians to come together on the first day of the week, to break bread and have fellowship. So we can follow this model for the principles behind our Sunday services.

We also learn from the early church that Church is as much defined by what goes on outside it as in what takes place inside. In the midst of the battles of life we can find peace inside the Church. When I go to church I think of myself as plugging into the power, authority and grace of the cross. But as Christians we are called to be in the world, though not held in its grasp, and problems start when men and women never want to come outside their church: they enjoy the comforts of fellowship and ministry too much! At church we should be getting strength, empowerment and encouragement - but for what purpose? Simply, to go back into the world to share the gospel and exercise its power.

This introverted mentality has meant that Christians have not released their energies into the world, but instead have turned them loose inside the Church, producing battles and strife. In this sense many Christians are like those we read about in the scriptures who received the Holy Spirit in Jerusalem. They wanted to make the city their home, to stay there within its blessed walls, to keep the Holy Spirit to themselves and get everyone else to come to them (Acts 2).

Instead, God in His goodness raised up Saul to persecute them and to scatter them far and wide. And then God saved Saul! If there wasn't persecution after Pentecost the Church could have stayed static in the upper room in Jerusalem. Persecution and Pentecost go together in the word of God as a symbol to us of the good things God wants us to receive by being rooted in our local church, but at the same time to teach us that we receive those

things in order to go back into the world, to bring the hope
and peace of Christ. Instead of wanting to fight, we must
learn that God's people should, refine each other 'as iron
sharpens iron' (Proverbs 27:17), allowing the Holy Spirit to
make us more like Christ as we have fellowship with one
another.

Evangelism and leadership

I had not long taken up my new position as pastor when I
began to feel that I was the proverbial lamb on its way to
slaughter. There was aggression and resentment from some
members of the church towards me as a young man in
leadership, which I felt I could never overcome. I was
labelled an 'evangelist' and not a pastor – a man in the
wrong job.

I didn't expect to meet those attitudes within the
church. My mind often drifted back to the way things used
to be. "I should have kept my job in the transport
company," I thought. Here I was, entrenched in leadership
and policy struggles in the church, when I had been used
to being the person who burst onto the scene, gave my all
to the local Christians for a week or two, then left,
returning to a safe place where I could be spiritually built-
up again.

It took only a few months to feel that I had been
conned. The outgoing pastor had known how tough it
would be for me to lead this church, and I wondered why
he hadn't told me. I was referred to as "the young pastor",
and believe me, that was not a compliment. I was not the
person that this church wanted to have as its leader and I
was aware of a good deal of silent criticism and the not-so-
silent circulation of names of other, more suitable,

candidates. The general attitude towards me and my strategies for the church was, it seemed to me, not an obstructive one but a non-cooperative one, and I felt sure that some of the elders and the congregation were waiting to see me fail.

There were exceptions. One elder, who I visited in his home, prayed for me, and I remember he said very clearly, "Young man, you are God's choice. Don't let any one tell you differently."

God also blessed me with a small group of young, gifted people in the church who wanted to support me and among whom there was a heart and mind for God. It was with these people that I planned and implemented changes in the church. With sensitivity and discretion I took strategies and proposals to the elders for endorsement rather than affirmation, and left the real decisions to be taken outside of the formal leadership group. I knew I couldn't convince them of the need for change and for redirection, and that to try would be to waste a huge amount of time and energy.

I knew that God could convince them though, and I had faith that not far into the future there would be signs of new fruit, of conversions and baptisms. When they could see growth and maturity in the church with their own eyes, I believed I would break through. And, praise God, within about a year and a half, we were seeing these things happening in the church.

As I saw it, part of my development as a good evangelist in the body of Christ, was to go through the difficulties of leading this particular church and learn about the strengths and weaknesses of church life. The attitude that I was first greeted with as the new leader – the mentality which said that my evangelistic ministry was next

to useless in terms of running a church and being a pastor–
was overturned as, by God's power, we began to see
change in the church.

I want to draw particular attention to the
compartmentalisation of spiritual gifts in the life of the
church which, I am sure, lay behind the way I was received
as a leader. In my vision for the church, evangelism was
not a secondary phase or spur of church life. For me, all
parts of church life are facilitated by evangelism. An
evangelism programme is not something to consider when
we have got other things sorted out. It is not a fringe
activity or a luxury. Evangelism is at the heart of a change
in attitude to the life of a church. Instead of saying that
teaching, training and pastoral care must be set in place
before outreach can begin, I led the church with the vision
that evangelism will bring these other parts of a healthy
church into fruition.

None of us can say that we have all the gifts: we
need one another in the church because God has given us
gifts, talents and abilities to complement each other. We
are not competing against one another, or trying to outdo
each other. The gifts are complementary and bring us into
unity (Ephesians 4:11-16). Evangelism brings holiness
because we cannot preach what we are not.

As I see it, good evangelism is much more than
going out and shouting at people that Jesus loves them.
Evangelism is about setting in place a whole structure of
teaching and pastoring which is ready to receive those
people who respond to the message. Evangelism will bring
the kingdom of God on earth.

Out of Africa

The first twelve months of leadership in this church were characterised by frustration and conflict. I wanted the people to follow me as I followed God, but it was like pushing an elephant uphill. Yet change was on the horizon, and it began with my first visit to Africa. This experience, in the second year of my pastorship, was the catalyst for change in my understanding of the congregation and their responsiveness to me.

I had for some time felt that there was a gap in my ability to fully relate to the majority of the congregation, who were Africans. I was aware that I was making mistakes, that all I could do when talking to them about Africa was to make generalisations. I knew there were many tribes, customs and languages, but I had no grasp of their heritage. I wanted to know what the style of worship was in their homeland and what the church there was like.

I had also begun to understand that a lot of cultural issues had surfaced in the problems of the early months of my leadership of the church. As I have said, having a pastor under the age of thirty was particularly difficult for Africans to accept, as they were used to much older men in church leadership. I had come to realise that their unhappiness at the situation was not actually vindictiveness but an expression of a conflict of cultures. As I had to understand this, and be sympathetic to it, they also had to learn to deal with it.

When word got around that I was planning the trip, some Ghanaians that I knew generously offered to pay the extra airfare for me to extend my visit from Nigeria to Ghana, and so with everything in place, I left with great anticipation. Four weeks was going to be a long time away from home, particularly as Louise, my wife, had recently given birth to our first child, Jake.

As the plane touched down I remembered my teenage years as a Rasta when Africa had been the land of dreams and fulfillment, a spiritual home I had longed for and sang about.

> Africa is paradise, is the land of the old and the young.
> Repatriation is a must, Selassie say he will take us home.
> Now, now, Back Jah, we are on the right side.
> Now, now, Back Jah.

Now I realised how emotional it was for me to come to Africa, not just because I had grown up with Africa in my head, but because of the higher purposes I had in my vision for church-building.

I came down to earth with a bang in those first moments at Nigeria's airport at Port Harcourt. The friends who were supposed to be meeting me were late and I was left in the hands of a hostile immigration officer, who confiscated my passport and demanded numerous examples of my signature. After I had been accused of coming into the country as a spy, my friends arrived, and it soon became evident that all the immigration official required was a swift backhander, and I was free to go.

Africa was not all good, as I had imagined, and my eyes slowly opened to the extremes of rich and poor in this country. I saw very big houses, I saw many Mercedes Benz cars. (In fact, I came to the conclusion that there were more Mercedes cars here than there were in London.)

I saw one particularly large house, and when I asked who lived there, I was told that its only occupant was its dead owner who was interred there. A large block of flats, which I assumed would have belonged to the government, actually belonged to one man. I began to realise that many of my congregation members back in England came from wealthy, middle class backgrounds.

Though I was shocked that this was the Africa I had dreamt about, I was soon excited at the prospect of meeting lots of Africans. As best as I could I learnt the words for "good morning", "good afternoon" and "good evening", as it was customary to greet one another even in passing on the streets. I wanted everyone to know that even though I was a stranger, I honoured and respected their culture.

I was greatly impressed and touched by the importance of the family network in African society and the support it provided. At one village elders' meeting, it was customary for the father of the family to be present, and if he was unable to attend, he delegated the responsibility to his eldest son, and if he could not go, then the next son took his place. I was even more surprised to find that the next day one family was visited and required to pay a fine because their family had not been represented at the meeting!

Families joined together in the early morning and again in the evening for times of devotion. A mid-week prayer meeting was attended by a thousand people! It was mind-blowing. The church services I went to were full of enthusiasm and joy, song and dance. On one occasion I was taken on a short drive to a church convention, and as we drove we passed many people making the journey on foot, carrying chairs and benches on their heads.

When we arrived, as far as the eye could see there were people, interspersed with many choirs. The service itself lasted for three hours, and believe me, it took another three hours to take up the offering. "What a mighty God we serve", was one vibrant song I particularly remember singing there.

The whole congregation was engaged in worship, in making melody to the Lord, and in dancing. I recall that I was very concerned for all the babies carried in slings on the backs of their dancing mothers – I was so sure they would fall out. And all the time I was amazed to think that this was the tradition that the people in my church in London had come from. I had always thought of them as subdued, and in contrast to this rich and powerful worship, that certainly seemed to have been true.

I couldn't wait to get home and to stir up some of this in my congregation. On my first Sunday back I addressed the familiar faces with the words, "All you Africans have backslidden." They looked at me.

"Okay, watch this," I said, and I raised a song I had heard in Nigeria, "Thank you for saving me. Thank you my Lord". I came to the front of the altar and clapped and danced the way I had seen it. Some Nigerian ladies came out and joined me, and I was so excited I said, "You've got to do this! This is you! I want to see this!" I had never before seen them express themselves before God in this way.

This was a significant turning point in the life of the church. People began to feel that they could express their cultural experience with freedom in worship. Until now they had had to fall in line with English traditions of worship. It was an important lesson to me that in the church, like elsewhere, people need to feel culturally accepted, and to know that they have a cultural contribution to make to the body of Christ.

Freedom and worship

For some time, members of the church had been meeting informally in people's homes for 'African Fellowship' evenings, and I was concerned to draw into our Sunday services the kind of things that were happening there. They were often all-night prayer meetings, with energetic clapping and worship. This was not happening in the wider context of the life of the church, and it was a great challenge for me to bring these two elements – the informal meeting style and the Sunday meeting style – together in an offering of praise to God, so that there would no longer be this fringe group which came in and out of the church without really connecting with it. I could only preach and teach these things, and reassure people that unity and diversity were two strong pillars of God's kingdom.

For many churches, the 1980s saw the rising popularity of worship songs as opposed to hymns, and the divergence that came in its wake, between those who preferred the traditional format and those who wanted to worship with songs and guitars. These choices had nothing to do with the cultural issues in church life which my congregation was facing, but they were another part of the wave of change approaching us. Singing choruses instead of, or as well as, hymns enabled people to be much more spontaneous in their worship. The ability to put the hymn book down and worship God with freedom was, and continues to be, a major change and challenge in our church life.

I loved hymns and always had one or two in our Sunday services, but I also wanted people to know liberty in the Spirit, to exercise giftings, and have the opportunity to hear from God. I wanted there to be space in the service, instead of the hymn-prayer sandwich, so that we could cry before God, so that those of us who had had a tough week could release it to God. There should be order in our meetings, but also liberty and spontaneity. Structure in the church can be good, but the structure is not there to hamper the gospel. The structure exists to complement what God is doing. Just as there is order in heaven, and order in scripture, there should be order on earth. But when the structure becomes a hindrance, frustration sets in and people get disillusioned.

The most important thing for me, before and after this visit to Africa in 1986, was that the church should be a place of passionate worship. If the question was asked, what was I really looking for – black culture-led worship or passionate worship – the answer was simple. My foremost desire was for whole-hearted worship, in which worshippers, whatever their colour, were in touch with God with their whole being.

As a child in my family church in north London, I thought there was more life in the local cemetery than there was in the church, and people still tell me similar things today. We need to move on from worship as an academic exercise, as it so often can be, to see the church vibrant in worship, with the hearts of its members engaged in love for God.

So it was from this starting point that I wanted to understand and value the cultures that people came from. After all, God has given us different cultures, and he wants us to express ourselves as individuals. We need to appreciate and value the traditions that our brothers and sisters are coming from. I wanted to lead the members of my congregation into an understanding of God's acceptance of each of us, and our individual expressions of praise and worship.

It weighed greatly on my mind, however, in the months following my return from Africa, that I was opening the way for a culture clash. How would the vision I had for my church affect its non-African members? The union of traditional British worship and the loud and expressive music of the African-Caribbean culture would surely be like a duet between the violin and the drum!

I soon began to see the consequences. After a short time, the style of worship in the church began to reflect the black majority in the congregation and sadly, the white folks found other churches to go to. Many times I was told that individuals or families were finding it a struggle to travel the distance to the church and had found a church nearer to home. I felt deeply that people's perception was that this church was getting to be a black African-Caribbean church. Yet I strove for the balance, to teach that there was good in all traditions, and to combine the congo drum with singing hymns.

Understanding tradition

It soon became apparent that the training I had received in college had been inadequate in terms of preparing me for leadership. I suppose I went in as a young and naïve leader, thinking I could lead the church, impact the community and reach out to the world. The reality was that I faced a lot of opposition from some of my leadership team and from many of the congregation themselves. I realised that I had quite a task on my hands just to address the issue of Tradition in the church. By this I don't mean any one custom or ceremony in particular, but the reverence that silently accrues to the traditional way of doing things among the leaders and members.

The undercurrent of obstinacy and the resistance to seeing God move in the church often took the form of financial issues. When I proposed open-air services the primary response I got was related to money and whether, if the meeting was outdoors, we would still be able to take an offering. Generally speaking, I found that it was easier to find money or agreement for maintenance of the fabric of the building than it was to plan a programme of outreach. This was a source of turmoil for me, because all I wanted to do was tell people about Jesus, and the creativity with which I wanted to do it was being stifled.

One suggestion I made was that we could hire a lorry with which to tour the locality, worshipping and giving the message of the gospel. For some in the congregation there was horror at the thought of what might befall the piano if we moved it onto the lorry, and comments were made about the desecration of church furniture. At this point grace was getting further and further away from me, and I had to ask the Lord for the grace to be a pastor to my congregation. I knew then, as I do now, that the real problem was Tradition, and I feel that this is a spiritual stronghold. In fact, I call it the "demon of tradition".

Tradition is still hampering the growth of many churches today. Many Christians are still looking back to what God did in their youth and in the days of their parents. Although God never changes, he is progressive in his works ('Behold I do a new thing', he says in Isaiah 43:19).

With this in mind, there is a very real need for emerging leaders to get maximum exposure to grass roots church life, the structure and the culture of the denomination, during their training. If this foundation is set in place, he or she will be better able in their thinking, praying and preparation, to find a strategy which will not scatter the flock, which will not cause people to feel that they have been sidelined.

Joshua was constantly at the side of Moses, seeing firsthand how difficult it was to lead the multitude of the Israelites. When he took over from Moses his declaration was, 'As for me and my house, we will serve the Lord' (Joshua 24:15). He had clarity and determination about what he was going to do which must have helped to protect him when other people pulled in different directions. I constantly remember one of my friends, now living in Africa, whose wisdom was very valuable in helping me with some very difficult decisions and hot debates in our elders' meetings. It is very important that young pastors have senior people who they can call on in times of difficulty.

I would say to leaders who are faced with tough decisions, that what a leader needs is a good heart and a right spirit. A good heart says, "I am not out to crush people, but to help people, to empathise with them and to understand where they are in their walk with God." A good leader is going to be sensitive and graceful in the ways they implement the vision that he or she feels the Lord is giving them. Good leadership can transform the thinking and traditions of the 'old guard' and bring new life, a new dynamic, new zeal and passion among people in the church. It is also important that the congregation knows that they have leaders who will lead them out to preach the gospel, to minister to the sick and get involved in social action.

A work of grace

Leaders, first and foremost, need God's grace. Grace allows us to realise that it takes time to get a mindset to change. It means that we have got to have patience, and be prepared for the long haul. It means that we must be ready to spend a lot of time negotiating with other people's points of view. A leader must listen and help people to see what they are talking about and where the Lord is leading. Where people are antagonistic, grace means that a leader should hold fast to the fact that as a pastor, they are still responsible for the spiritual development of their congregation.

Grace means that sometimes a leader will have to give up his or her convictions for a season in order to help people reach the point where the vision can be picked up again and the church can move on. Grace also means that leaders will accept the fact that they lose some battles and win some.

I know that my hope is in God's gifts of grace and patience, and I know I need them in every circumstance. Church life is about relationship, and having to work at relationships. As Paul put it to the Corinthians, we have to die daily to ourselves and our human will in order to let God have his way through and in us (1 Corinthians 15:31). Knowing there will be conflicts in church life, leaders need to ask God to help them deal with it day by day, to keep them from reacting to it, and to stay focused on his heart.

When grace is flowing, people's views and traditions will be transformed. What we all like about our traditions is that we feel comfortable with them. Therefore leadership often involves asking people to step out of that comfort zone and become open to the unknown. It takes time, prayer and a lot of grace to move some people in this way. We have to bear in mind that not everybody will receive the vision and conviction at the same time, so there has to be a flow of God's grace so that leaders are able to stand back and realise that some of their flock are at one stage and some are at another.

One particular issue I had to deal with was an organisation called The African Student Movement, which I felt had passed its sell-by-date, but nonetheless, was very dear to many people. It took two years before I could begin to close this group down. I met with fierce opposition, but said to people that if God wanted it to continue it would. So although, as leader, I could have reined it in at any time, I let it run on because for some of the people at that point, there was a strong emotional tie to this movement. Sometimes things like this are so strongly loved by people that a church may lose a few members over it. I knew that as a pastor it was vital that I did everything in my power to make sure that my brothers and sisters knew that to close the movement was not a vindictive act, but the result of its failure to function in a useful way.

Communicating the vision

There are several ways in which leaders can communicate their vision. Number one is through teaching from the Bible. Pastors need to know what the Bible says about the

Church. What is the role and responsibility of the Church? The purpose of the Church is to bring glory and honour to its head, Jesus Christ, as we try to live like Jesus, share his gospel, love people and care for them through social action.

My second point is timing. A church should remember that the vision is always for an appointed time. When I read Luke chapter 4 ('The Spirit of the Lord is on me...'), I have to remind myself that that scripture was prophesied 750 years before! (Isaiah 61:1-2) A leader should not be looking to drive his or her congregation, but to say to God, "When is the time, when is the season, for this vision to come to fruition?"

I learnt from those difficult relationships with the elders in the early years of my ministry, that it is best not to bring too many things to the agenda at one meeting, because you may frighten some people! Sharing a vision can be very overwhelming if a person cannot see what you are seeing. Therefore, at times, it is far easier to share little by little.

Undoubtedly, being a church leader is challenging. In its broadest sense, it is a difficult because a leader might only sow and never reap. He or she may find that like Moses, they can see the promised land, but they do not enter it. A minister or leader has to be active on the shop floor, but exert a strong presence in the boardroom as well. One of the greatest things I have learnt is to lead by example. Never expect other people to do things that I myself am not doing.

Jesus taught that the good shepherd leaves the ninety-nine and goes after the one. All leaders are called to care for people and to be responsible for them, to love them, and even though we may sometimes feel anger towards them, to constantly show grace. When I talk about owning people spiritually, I'm talking about loving them and praying for them on a daily basis, and being concerned for their lives and their welfare. Leadership is not just about management, it's about knowing that your congregation is the flock of God and Jesus has made you an under-shepherd.

Four

BUILDING FOR
GROWTH

It took about three years for me to say with assurance that God was doing something through my life, and that largely came about through the realisation that as an evangelist and church leader, I was in a position to get this church doing evangelism! I had more or less the final say in the overall programme of the church, its finance and the structure of its services, and of course, this was a great opportunity! I thought, "Praise God, this is really great!" I knew that God was using my evangelism ministry to motivate and envision a church, and at the same time, he was teaching me about the work and ministry of a pastor. I was both exercising, and being trained in, the gifts. After the struggles and doubts of the first year in church leadership, it was a joy to see myself helping, complementing and blessing the church to get to grips with evangelism.

I also sensed that the attitude of the elders towards me had changed. They saw people being baptised – so many baptisms, in fact, that I hardly had time to dry out – and increased numbers coming to church. They couldn't deny that the power of God was evident in the church and that God's hand was upon me. Working through the structures of the church was the biggest challenge I had experienced in the move from itinerant evangelism to the role of pastor. On the street or in a pub I was simply led by my heart to see people saved. In my church, major changes had to be negotiated through the elders, and together the leadership needed to be continually informed of the overall strategy for the church.

As a leader I was no good at cajoling people and moving people around to get things how I wanted them, but I had learnt that I needed diplomacy, sensitivity and the ability to talk to others. Unchanged however, was my desire to share my heart, and my heart was motivated by love for God, a passion for the gospel, and a burden to see people saved.

The church was growing, praise God, and within two years we were cramped in our building. When God begins to move we need to prepare the ground for expansion and change, physical and spiritual. A church needs men and women in leadership who are planning ahead and thinking strategically about growth. In our case, we required a release of finance if we were to expand our premises and keep abreast of changes. However, on this front we were restricted by the structure of the denomination. The message from the denomination was clear: growth was fine and more money coming in was fine, but there was no flexibility as to the money that was due to the central funds, and nothing more would be given to meet the demands of a congregation that was now reaching four hundred worshippers on a Sunday.

Churches need to have systems in place so that whenever growth takes place, they have the means to resource it. Many churches are stagnant and not growing, yet they are still maintained, so how much more important is it that church denominations have a structure that says, "When you grow, we can accommodate and encourage"?

Uncorking the wine

As the church saw these signs of new life and growth, I recognised that many Christians were experiencing an excitement and fervour within the four walls of the church building, but when they got outside, it was as if everything became bottled up. One of my thoughts was that if I could get our folks to do some of the things that were becoming part of our normal Sunday meetings *outside* the church, it would release them in their day-to-day living as Christians. Not only that, but people outside the church would be able to see, hear and understand that Christianity is exciting, relevant, and spiritually alive: we can all be connected to God!

My foremost desire was to see Christians sharing their faith. I clearly remember the apprehension on the faces of many of the congregation as we prepared for our first open-air service; they really looked uncertain about doing it. When I asked, if there was anyone who wanted to give their testimony, there was even more hesitation. I realised though, that this was quite natural. I had been doing this for years, but it was a new thing for many of them. It was a challenge for me to know how best to deal with this. Instead of asking for a testimony, I started by asking for a small group who would be happy to sing a hymn. Alternatively, I would interview someone, which was less threatening as I would stand with them at the front, and the short question-and-answer format was reassuring.

The first time we did this, many local people came out of their houses or onto the balconies of their flats. Some even joined in with the singing, and when the church folks saw this, their excitement grew. 'Doing' evangelism was a lot more encouraging to people than sitting in church talking about it.

I was able to say to people, "Hey guys, we have been talking about evangelism, praying about it and fasting, now we're going to do it. And people out there do want what you have." When they saw people in the crowd listening and joining in, it inspired them to greater confidence.

We also saw other reactions, and I recall one occasion when I was preaching with a lady called Edith and some eggs were thrown at us. Surprisingly, this actually had a positive spin-off, showing the church that taking our message to people can be costly. For many of the folks, it was encouraging because they knew that the apostles they read about in the books of Acts and Corinthians also went through persecution for their faith.

So taking the church outside the church building helped individuals greatly. They were able to see that they had shared their faith on Sunday, now they needed to do it all through the week. They knew they needed to invite their friends and continue with this because it was challenging and good.

One particularly significant event I remember came about in response to a festival that was taking place in a park opposite our church. On the same day, the church had planned a special evening service for people to bring their friends to, which was to be led by a group of students from Youth With A Mission, who were going to perform a play based on the Genesis account of God's creation, called "Toymaker and Son".

After praying and thinking about this event, I met with the elders about ten minutes before the six o'clock service, and I asked them, "Could we take this play and the gospel service to the festival?" They raised objections, ranging from the practicalities of taking up the offering, to what we would do about the people who might turn up at the church for the first time and find it closed. But in the end we picked up our chairs, and over a hundred people came to our service at the festival, watched the play and heard me preach, and some of them were saved. It showed us all that we must listen and hear what God is saying to his people.

A receptive church

The foundation for church growth and for the church coming alive to evangelism, is preparation for the simple fact that there will be change: the time of our service, its contents, and its order, and the very people you sit next to, will change. One of the biggest problems in church life, is that people pray for revival – they ask God for souls to be won – but they are not ready for it.

I was certain that God would bring the wind of change sweeping through our church and I wanted to raise expectation levels among the congregation. To this end, one Sunday, in the hour or so before everyone else arrives at church (the time when the pastor does vital jobs like making sure the boiler is working), I changed the layout of all the chairs in the building. By the time I had finished, where once the chairs had faced the front of the church and the pulpit, they now faced towards the right hand side.

I am sure I had a good idea of the kind of reaction I would get, but went ahead anyway because I wanted it to serve as a visual aid – an illustration of our response to change. Suffice to say that most of the congregation were upset. There were cries of "Where is my seat?" and "Where do I sit now?" The elders were also unhappy and wanted to know why the rearrangement had taken place. Before the meeting could go ahead that day, I had to agree that by next Sunday the chairs would be returned to their normal place. However, in my sermon I made a point of drawing everyone's attention to the fact that it was very easy to get comfortable – in a job, in a marriage, in a church. I said to the congregation, "You were shocked weren't you? Well, God is going to shake us up. There will be a time when there will be so many people in here that you won't just be unable to find your seat, you won't get a seat at all!"

Evangelism brings change and radically affects the dynamics of a church. Growth will come from constantly seeking to develop our churches as places where people will be challenged, and as places where we make it known that the God we serve is a limitless God. Our church planning needs to be projected – we need to understand where God is leading us. All too often we are caught up in events, and dictated to by events, and it is not until after the whirlwind has passed that we are ready for it. We need to preach about the second coming of the Lord, but we also need to prepare men and women for the events of today and tomorrow. We don't know when the Lord is going to come so we need to prepare and project for the future.

Growth brings with it major implications for churches, and too often we are reactive not proactive. We often pray, "Lord, send us people. Lord, send us revival", but before we say "Amen!" we need to think through the implications of change, and get ready for it. Going from a congregation of fifty people to one of a hundred and fifty is a big change, and it will have a dramatic effect on a church's needs in pastoral care, visiting, leadership, home groups, children's work and worship. All church leaders should be thinking about the implications of growth, and more than this, be preaching and teaching about preparation for change in our churches.

So leaders should prepare their congregations for change; prepare them to get to know the issues in terms of where people are, how they might live their lives, and the whole range of things they might believe. It's good to have a structure that will cater for Mums, for Dads, for single parents, for children, for people who are going through marital problems, for alcoholics, for people of different racial backgrounds, for those with social problems, for people with problems in terms of their sexuality.

As I led my congregation I began to talk about all these issues, stressing that we live in the real world, and that the church has to be part of it. If our doors are going to be truly open, we have to be able to minister to all kinds of people. I find that this is an ongoing problem for Christians – the knowledge that once they start to preach the gospel they are going to touch many lives, and that they must to be prepared to minister to those lives.

The problem is illustrated all too clearly by the cliques of people sometimes found in church. One of the questions I asked of my congregation was, "After the service is finished, who do you talk to first? Is it a friend, a deacon, the church secretary, someone in your home group you need to touch base with, or is it a stranger?" Non-Christians are spiritual people too; they are able to discern, and when they come to church for the first time, they want to know whether the people there are loving, caring and welcoming.

They ask themselves, "How was I received? Did anyone take note of me, or approach me?" They are looking for these things, just as the Christian on the 'inside' is. I suggested to my congregation that instead of immediately going to a friend after the Sunday meeting, they greeted someone they didn't know. Tell them about yourself, I encouraged, and find out about them. It's a question of interaction. In addition to this, I do believe a pastor should stand at the door if possible, and welcome people, making a special effort to say, "Hi, how are you?" Then newcomers have some point of contact.

Understand your audience

Every congregation needs to think how it can serve the community spiritually, socially and practically. I very much wanted our church to be locally focused so that it could put its community first, and be the focal point of that community. As a leader I found I had a lot to do to educate people's thinking, so as part of our preparation for growth and readiness to receive new people, I instigated seminars and training on the social, historical and religious issues that gave our community its identity.

I asked myself, "What are the needs of this community?" I firmly believe that if you want to serve the place where you live, you need to know it; you need to get out there, walk around on a Saturday night, Sunday afternoon, on weekdays, to see what is going on. That is what I did.

It is possible to go fishing and find that there are no fish in the pond. I didn't want to be catering for an age group or a specific social group that didn't exist in our area. Churches need to be focused in their outreach, and that is why I spent time at the town hall and the library making use of information which is accessible to everyone, and more often than not, is used to target the junk mail that we all get through our doors. I feel that it is difficult to pray effectively and intelligently, and plan strategically for the needs of our community, unless we study and pray over this information.

In particular, I visited the primary and secondary schools to meet the headteachers and introduce myself, and I asked them how the church could be of any help to them. I met youth club leaders, to see how they were meeting the needs of the young people in the area. I went into pubs, met the landlords, and told them who I was, why I was here, and I found out if there was anything the church could do for them.

Another way in which I got to understand my community was to organise a survey of the borough in which the church was situated. To my amazement, I discovered that our locality had the highest rate of single parent families in the country, as well as one of the highest drop-out rates from education. It was after that that I began to realise that if we wanted to reach our community, we ought to think about providing nursery facilities and education facilities in the church building.

I drafted a feasibility study for the church's proposals in this area. I didn't want a church that would close its doors from one Sunday to the next, maybe opening again for its midweek Bible study. I believe it should be open to the community, *for* the community, as well as being a place of worship. It is not the building that is the most important thing, the building is there to serve the people.

I had no problem with the idea that we use the church during the week as a gym, or a youth club, because it was serving the community. Back in the West Indies, I had known of a church that had been class one, two, three and four of the local school. It became a church again for a wedding on a Saturday and for the meeting on a Sunday. As far as our church in London went, we needed to build something in which we could cater for the whole person.

The aim was that we would have a nursery for forty children as well as running a Saturday School and a homework club. I was already working closely with local schools, and as a church we wanted to develop this. I would occasionally get called in to help resolve problems in the nearby school, and had also been on weekends away with teachers and children. As I saw it, there should be bridges from the church to the community, and from the community into the church, and I wanted people to be constantly crossing those bridges.

I once led a group of students onto the streets in Birmingham, and the remit I gave them was not to make converts but to walk the area around their church with a questionnaire. I gave them two questions to present to their community: one, "Do you know our church?" and two, "What do you think our church should be doing for the community?" Lastly, they were to take the opportunity to tell members of the public what the church *was* doing and give them details of its various programmes and meetings.

They discovered that although their church was on a main road and very prominent, few people really were aware of it. Most interestingly, the conversations they had with people opened-up a huge catalogue of social needs and areas in which local people wanted the church to be involved. Many of the students that day heard how bored young people were, how there was nowhere for them to go which would be safe and free from drugs. Others told them that there were many people in the neighbourhood with mental health needs. They were asked, "What is your church doing about mental health?"

All these are real and big issues: a church must get the right people in place to deal with them, and have the

church finances to make a difference. This particular group
of students came back overwhelmed by the needs they had
heard people talking about, and many of them asked,
"Where do we start?" Simply, we have to get back to the
Church's need to have a burden for its community. A
burden and a vision. Out of that comes prayer, an analysis
of our strengths and weaknesses, listening to God, and
slowly building up from the things we know we can do,
and growing into the areas that are more challenging.

The church exists for the whole person, not just
the spiritual, and so although it operates out of a Christ-
centred ethos, at the end of the day Christians shouldn't
force the gospel down people's throats, but they should
want to help them to understand what Christianity is all
about. So when I go into schools, according to the 1948
Education Act, I cannot seek converts on the school
premises, but I can present the case for salvation. I can
present the case that God wants young people to prosper
academically, to help themselves and their communities,
and God also wants them to be receptive spiritually to the
gospel.

When people genuinely see our concern for the
whole person, and they know who we are and what we
stand for, they are generally receptive, and they can choose
whether to come to church or not. So in this area, I did not
meet with much opposition, because people could see that
the church was giving to the community rather than taking
its money and staying irrelevant to people's lives. As a
church we have no right to ask people for money if we are
not going to do something with it socially, practically and
spiritually.

One year we had a harvest festival service and
people brought food and laid it before the altar. Local

school children then took the food gifts to elderly people in the community, as a gesture of friendship between the young and the old. Then we gave the school a financial gift for their funds, and the church's relationship with the school really took off. Later in the year we offered the church building to the school for its Christmas service, and both the school and the congregation were impressed and blessed by the interdependence that had been established. It had a positive effect on the church because by broadening its perspective it helped us to see that our gospel is an holistic one. We could see that if we were contributing practically to the community, people would respond to us and our message.

The Church's cutting edge

Working with the Local Authority can be daunting, but as Christians and as a Church we cannot afford not to be involved. That's where decisions are being taken which will affect our parishoners, our members, our communities, and we need to be part of the discussions on housing, on education, and policing. As I see it, it is part of a local minister's responsibility to be involved in the processes of local government in the community, whether that be politics or social action.

As our church had started by looking at the needs of the borough, we were able to present these facts to the Local Authority at the same time as presenting to them our vision for the area. Having presented the feasibility study, which was well received, it became clear that we were on a very long road of negotiation and communication with the Council in order to be approved for funding for the building and development projects that centred on our church. It was very difficult to get answers about how our case was progressing, and at which stage of the various committees it was. We knew our application was being favourably looked on and that the Council had been impressed with our proposals, but even after we knew that we would be given the money, there was still a long way to go, through planning procedures, the details of finances for running the nursery, and building regulations.

I found the to and fro of paperwork quite tedious. Months went by and we didn't hear anything from the Council. Then, suddenly, they would contact us with a request for something that they needed straight away! Yet when we wanted something from them it was very difficult to get any response. It was a trying time, but in the end it was very profitable.

History shows us that groups like the Salvation Army and the Shaftesbury Society have played a crucial part in our cities, and yet, sadly, everybody recognises that since the second world war the Church has lost its edge in terms of its social action. The more the nation became prosperous in the Fifties, the more the Church lost members. The new levels of wealth produced a desire for independence from the Church. A certain stigma also became attached to Christian organisations. Wealth brings riches for rich people but it also brings poverty for poor people, and the Church as a whole lost touch with the fact that it had a social role to play.

As the Church became complacent and lost its conviction, its traditional responsibilities were taken over by the government through The Beveridge Report and the advent of the Welfare State. However, it was not long before governments slackened off their social commitments, which were supposed to belong to the

Church and charitable organisations once more. However, the Church ignored its responsibilities to society in favour of preaching heaven all the time.

Local Authorities are always on the look out for churches that are stimulating a healthy community; they warm to the church when it has policies that embrace education, childcare, housing, and youth clubs. Councils want to plug into what the Church is doing so that at the end of the day the community can be properly and effectively run in terms of policy and strategy, and properly cared for in terms of people's social needs.

Like the rest of the community, the Council with which I was dealing wanted, first and foremost, to be confident that our church was not a fly-by-night set-up. When the authorities recognise that churches are permanent organisations with a heart for, and a commitment to, the community and, most importantly, they see that we are credible, then we will find that when there are crucial decisions to be made, they will respond to us. Local Authorities are always cautious, but we have got to build relationships, we've got to build trust. We have got to let them know why we're there. In the end, whether it takes two, three or five years, it is worth it. The responsibility of local government is to make sure their policies are impacting the community, and they know that it is a grass-roots organisation like a church that will help them to be constructive and effective in achieving that.

The Council agreed to give us £280,000, of which the majority went towards the rebuilding programme at the church. The remainder was earmarked for the salaries involved in setting up the nursery and Saturday School. During my time as congregation leader, these finances were raised and the proposals agreed, and a management

committee was set in place whose job it was to appoint a
nursery manager and the other staff that would be needed.
Credibility and reliability are crucial when any organisation
is looking to raise funds. People want to know that our
biblical perspective will tally up with the needs of the
community, and that the community will see some benefit
from the finances.

Our responsibility is not just to preach the gospel
but to make sure that people can *feel* the power of the
gospel. This might mean going to a family where a child
has just dropped out of school, and talking and praying
with them, and encouraging the child to go to school; or to
deal with the teenager who has got pregnant, and to be
able to offer a nursery place for her baby so that the
mother's education can be continued. These are the things
that make us genuine and credible, and are the fulfilment
of the gospel in us.

The holistic gospel

It was very important for us as we 'rebuilt' our church to
look carefully at what we were trying to build. Were we just
seeking a nice building for Sunday morning worship, or
were we going to build something that would reflect the
kingdom of God and the holistic gospel that we believed
in? I felt very much that the new building had to reflect the
social, spiritual and educational needs of the community.
My heart was for it to be a place of worship, a place of
education and care, a place where people could come for
leisure activities.

One of the biggest challenges for the Church as we
move into the twenty-first century, is to be relevant to the
whole person. We will struggle if we don't reflect the needs

of our community in our preaching, within our social action, even in the context of the buildings that we have. For me, the church we were rebuilding was going to be a place where mothers could say that their children went to nursery; where children came for an education at Saturday school or Sunday School; where others could say that it was the place where I met Jesus and became a Christian; where pensioners could come for special events and away days; or where kids could come for a football tournament.

The church would then be an accessible focal point for the community, to rival the pub. Whether it's a jobshop or a place for Sunday worship, there is something there for everyone, and people are saying, "I have to go there at least three times a year for something!"

Growing leaders

One of the Church's major weaknesses has always been a shortage of leaders and a failure to produce people who are able to pastor or work alongside a pastor in leadership. Leaders have got to think of their own development in terms of spiritual maturity. I should not say to myself that the way I think now, and the ministry I have now, will be the same in five years time. Christians need to live in the light of the fact that God has greater challenges for us, because many times the problems of change and development originate with those who have responsibility and authority in the church.

As leaders we must train the next generation, so that in five years time they are ready to carry responsibility. They may be a baby today, but tomorrow they will be a mature adult with something to contribute to the further development of the kingdom. So not only do we need to develop today's leaders to take on these challenges, but we need to teach Christians about their responsibilities, their commitment, and their obligation in terms of the Church's growth and outreach.

I have always believed that none of us are indispensable. We have got to be like Paul and Timothy, making full use of our ministry, seeking to bring out the giftings that God has given us (1 Timothy 4:13-16). As a leader, I am always looking out for people who complement my giftings, who can help me. I ask myself, "Who are the people that will succeed me, who are the people I need to mentor so that in years to come they will be able to take on some new responsibility?" This is always on my heart and mind, because the church is not producing leaders quickly enough. So at the same time as we seek new converts, we work to develop leaders.

Humanly speaking, it is very difficult to keep track of people and their development and giftings in this way. We find that Moses tried to do everything, until Jethro, his father-in-law, made him realise that it was not possible for one man to judge every little problem among his people. Moses came to see that he had to find elders, men who were filled with God's spirit who could help him (Exodus 18:13-26). That is why every good leader is never totally responsible for everything. They may be responsible for the whole picture, but not every detail. They have other people, at many other levels, and with other giftings and abilities, helping to bring everything together.

In the area of maintaining growth, the most important thing is to have the right people in the right place. We need to develop people who will, with prayerful consideration, be in the right roles to maintain growth, without being overburdened. It is often the case that

Christian workers are so busy in their churches that they haven't got time to make relationships with their neighbours or non-Christian friends. It is very easy to fall into the trap of allowing this to happen, and I always try to watch out for it.

When God blesses a church and the church is growing rapidly – faster than it is able to train leaders – there will always be people who are overworked and overstretched. That is another reason that I stress the preparation of leaders. Sometimes the church can be likened to a building with its front door wide open, but the back door open even wider. When a church is running on empty, with over-busy people in the congregation, it might be able to give the impression that this is a great church, where there's a lot going on, but people are left wondering whether they are really loved there. The number one thing people are looking for in a church, is that it is a place where they are loved. It is good to have a large church, but at the end of the day, you may find there are more people leaving than there are joining.

The statistics show that about eighty per cent of Christians are inactive in their church, and it is generally a small number who carry the burdens of responsibility. It is important for us to have good structures and good team spirit, so that everyone can enjoy their work for the church, but it is also important that we have time to develop relationships with non-Christians. I remember looking at a notice board in one church and seeing that there was a church activity for every day of the week, and so I asked, "When do you have time to socialise with your family and friends?" The church member I was talking with laughed, but it is a serious thing. It is helpful to examine the level of responsibilities we give to those active in the church, so that there is balance.

I think that leaders often underestimate the giftings and ministries that individuals have in our churches. They tend have a stereotype in their mind of the kind of people they are looking for to take responsibility. When you think of Jesus and the twelve disciples that he picked, many of us would have problems choosing some of them today. Take for example, Peter, Simon the Zealot, or Judas, a charlatan, looking for the money. Would we have chosen them? Jesus did. There are people in our congregations that may not be the world's best communicators, or of high intelligence, but with a heart to serve God, the Holy Spirit, and with availability and willingness, we will be amazed how God will use these people. As leaders this is another area that we need to pursue.

Our first criteria should not be a person's educational background or the length of time they have been in the church, but whether or not they have got a heart for God. We can go back to Samuel the prophet who was looking for a future king for Israel. Top of his list of qualities and characteristics was stature, IQ, clothing and eloquence. God said to him, 'Man looks at the outward appearance, but the Lord looks at the heart' (1 Samuel 16:7). We need to learn from that. God is looking for men and women who are humble, and whose heart is available for service. As we prepare for the future of our churches we need to look for people like this and utilise them.

As our church was growing in the late 1980s, I began to plan for the future, thinking that if we are growing at this rate, how many pastors and leaders will I need in five years time? Where did we need to plant new churches? What kind of finances will we need in two years time if we have planted a church? Perhaps we should put some money aside now? The next generation need to be prepared for church life and for the social and ethical issues of the day. It is important that we have our finger on the pulse in our teaching, preaching and overall strategy.

Planting with good seed

People were coming to our church from different communities across the capital, and so it became more evident that now was the time to church plant. We now had nine cell groups meeting midweek, and so several 'openings' in terms of location presented themselves. We looked at our geographical make-up, and the areas of west and northwest London, particularly Chiswick, came up most often, and we decided to go for that locality. The challenge for us was to get the right leader in there, and we thought we had the right person living in north London, on a convenient route for west London.

We launched the church plant with a lot of enthusiasm. We knew that it would take some time for the daughter church to really get going, but we were confident that the thirty to forty people who were moving into the new church would form a strong nucleus, and others would join them. However, although I thought we were prepared for this important development, we weren't. The church plant was premature, and after a period of two years it was recalled, and the church tasted failure.

The first mistake was that the appointed leader had a demanding full-time job outside the church, and after a while he wasn't able to be consistent as his job took him out of London. Difficulties also arose because this leader didn't live in the community in which the new church was based. He lived a few miles away, and this, I believe, was a significant problem. People with families also found it difficult to get to the church for meetings during the week, because many of them also did not live in the immediate locality. In time, others who were active members moved out of the area for a variety of reasons. Clearly, if you plant a church, you have to make sure that the main body of those who move with the plant are committed to it for a number of years. If within eighteen months people begin to move on, it has serious consequences for the enthusiasm of the local community and those that they leave behind in the church.

Although the plant started promisingly, as time went by the numbers dwindled, the leader became over-burdened and the mother church was not able to put enough time and resources into establishing the plant. The hardest thing was to acknowledge that the plant was not working.

I had time to reflect on this at a conference in New Zealand that I attended in 1988. I listened to a speaker whose subject was church planting and evangelism, and many of the things he touched upon rang true and crystallised the problems for me. I then had to convince the leadership that the plant wasn't working, and that we needed to pull it back in. It is better to act quickly in these situations, as those who have been involved with the daughter church can become demoralised and feel unable to be committed to any subsequent plant, or even to the main congregation itself.

Once you plant out a church, people get an enthusiasm for it; they own it and get a feeling of independence. It is very easy to plant out, but it's very difficult to bring it back in because sometimes, unfortunately, rather than seeing that they are part of a wider vision, a spirit of independence takes over, and people get very emotional about closing the church down. In the midst of that, the church loses people. More damage can be done by church planting if you get it wrong, than can be achieved successfully if you get it right.

It actually took years to close this new church, although it should have been folded within two. It was very hard to convince its members and leaders that they should return to the main church and they, in turn, felt that they weren't getting enough resources from the mother church. This lengthy period of unsolved decline had its casualties. People felt let down and emotionally drained, and many of them struggled with the concept of coming back to the original church, and as a consequence, many of them didn't.

One major reason for planting out as we did was because the church was bursting at the seams, but this in itself is not a good enough reason. We were like a woman who gets pregnant, but thinks only of the conception and pregnancy, and not of the child's life. I learnt the hard way that when a church plants out, it must do so with some of its best, key people. I reflected on the strong nucleus which I thought had been in place for the plant, and I came to the conclusion that fifty, at least, is a good number.

I recognised that a church plant needs a team of people who are ready to be involved and ready to take responsibility; too much emphasis placed on one person is not healthy. To be successful in church planting, the leadership has to be right. Finding motivated and envisioned people to go with the leaders is not always easy. Many Christians prefer to be where the action is – where there is service with a smile and where there are few demands on them. In a church plant each person has to stand up and be counted; everybody has a part to play. Not all are ready for this. There are those who want to go to church each week and enjoy Jesus, and have no motivation for the demands of planting out.

Leaders must count the cost before they launch a church plant. They must look at all the dynamics and all the implications. It is not enough that your church building is full up on a Sunday. Yet while Jesus tarries, until He comes again, we've always got to try, and try again, and learn from our failures.

Five

THE CHURCH AS COMMUNITY

I have always wanted to be part of a church that is impacting every part of society, every race and people group in the community. Yet when I looked around my congregation, I saw that at least ninety-five per cent of them were black, and I had to ask myself why. I believe strongly that God's kingdom is not black or white, but God's people living and worshipping together. I am not a naïve person, and I know that people are conscious of their colour and race, and yet the gospel transcends both.

The cross of Jesus embraces all colours and all races. So for me the challenge was, why aren't other racial groups coming to this church? Certainly, our church must have been giving the impression that it was the place to come for a certain style of worship because I recall that there were some that visited us not to worship but to watch how the locals worshipped. A group of students, whom I had come into contact with through my work in universities, came to the church, and it was as if they had a preconceived idea of what should, or would, happen. I think they thought it would be like something out of the Blues Brothers. When they didn't see that they were disappointed.

I began to ask myself, "What is culture?" I needed to understand this, and to communicate it to others. For example, how could we make room for cultural expression in worship, and at the same time have a worship style within which every person felt welcome and could identify with Christ? For me, that was, and is, the challenge. We must learn that if we are going to embrace the whole community, we have to be sensitive to racial issues, acknowledge that there are other cultures, and seek to encourage those cultures to participate in our services.

Kingdom culture

How important is it to value different cultural backgrounds in today's Church? Let me begin by saying there are many multi-racial, multi-cultural churches in the world. The progression that I am looking for, is an appreciation of diversity which goes beyond skin colour and place of origin. Churches need to be places where diversity is appreciated and incorporated.

We all need to ask, "How do I help others to be part, not of my culture, nor of their culture, but of *our* culture — a kingdom culture?" This is a culture that acknowledges biblical principles, practices and requirements, but is open to the variety of human expression that each culture brings to Christendom. The kingdom culture says primarily that we are all equally valued children of God — all different — but equal. Therefore, as we come before God and each other, there should be a liberty to be our true selves, in expression and as complimentary contributors to the life of the church.

My trip to Ghana in 1986 made me realise that the Africans in my church back home in London had had no alternative but to assimilate the dominant culture, and that did not bring out the best in them. It's alright to identify with the dominant culture, but there needs to be room for other cultural expressions too.

The things I learnt on that break from London church life enabled me to bring some degree of cultural release to my congregation when I returned, and it was a lesson that is still clear in my mind. In the kingdom of God we have to recognise the difference between kingdom culture and earthly culture; but we are still on earth, and we need to balance the two and find a common place to express that culture, where we know our individuality *and* our togetherness.

The Bible shows us that God gave Israel some basic principles about how to do things – principles that were meant to be handed down from generation to generation. God put in place rules that became cultural practices for the Israelites, because after so many years in Egypt they had lost their sense of identity as a group of people.

Culture is not wrong. In Deuteronomy, God effectively instructs the Israelites to establish for themselves cultural distinctives. Culture includes established traditions, values, morals and social behaviour patterns. This encompasses religious practices, festivals, social habits, upbringing, teaching and diet, all of which are spoken of in Deuteronomy from chapters 12-26.

The problems for the Israelites began not when they were on their own, but when they began to mix. For example, as the Israelites were about to move into Canaan they were specifically warned about the abhorrent cultural and religious practices of the Canaanites. God knew that by association there would inevitably be potential for a degree of assimilation of that culture, particularly since the Canaanites were the dominant culture. God did not want this because he knew that this association would undermine some of the most important cultural distinctives he had established in his people – worship and moral behaviour.

In the book of Deuteronomy we see that the Israelites do indeed discard their cultural distinctiveness and the things which God had said made them special to himself. I'm not saying that mixing is bad, but what happens (and this is as relevant today as it was for the

Israelites), is that when you pull some of another culture in, the tendency is to disregard some elements of your own culture in order to accommodate the other culture. Some good and relevant things of your own are lost, and turmoil sets in. This was the issue for the Israelites and is the issue for us.

Worshipping God is 'kingdom culture', but the expression of worship also reflects human cultures. Every culture reflects aspects of God's person and character as well as aspects of our fallen humanity. God gave Israel its culture, and consequently its identity. He gave the Israelites the opportunity to develop cultural practices (sometimes influenced by nearby people groups), and then he modified, prohibited or invested similar actions with new meanings (for example, sacrificing animals).

God calls for distinctiveness within our culture, traditions and heritage so that we remember who we are before him, and so that we are able to reject the demonised elements of our heritage and embrace that which reflects diversity in God. So culture is not wrong. It's important. When we look at people coming together in a multi-cultural church context, the question for every church leader is, to what extent are people coming in with good elements of their background culture, and being expected to discard or disregard it in order to take on the host culture? If this is happening, they are clearly not being encouraged to value and use those elements of their background culture that would benefit the body of Christ. Every church needs to evaluate this honestly. I am aware of the fact that culture is not static but is constantly changing, however, the issue of 'distinctiveness' is an important one.

What is culture?

Culture is one of those words which is used most often, in many contexts, with an assumed shared understanding of its meaning. However, I feel it is a word that we must necessarily unpack to ensure clarity, and a full appreciation of its central, foundational role in the life of individuals and communities. Culture is learned behaviour – behaviour taught to a child in their early years by significant community members. Children are taught what is valuable and acceptable to the community, and therefore, what should be valued by them as an individual.

This learning includes traditions, appropriate ways of behaving, for example, male and female roles. It also covers dress codes, music, food. The individual grows in identity from this important cultural foundation, and it is therefore so fundamental and integral to them that most people are not even aware of it.

When we go beyond skin colour, we open up the need to recognise the different ways – across cultural groups – that people worship, or the ways that people organise themselves, or the ways they relate to each other. This includes the way they deal with problems, the ways they resolve differences, and the way they express themselves.

Vive la différence

On returning from Ghana, the first thing I felt I had to do was to help people value their own cultures – to acknowledge and affirm them. And besides this, to get them to realise that people outside their own culture were equally valuable.

Being open to different cultural ways of doing things allows access to valuable and vital tools, keys if you like, to making relationships work anywhere, not just in a church. More than this, there are good things to be borrowed from one culture that will benefit another. I want to stress the importance of the principle of valuing and learning from each other.

We become acutely aware of our cultural heritage, however, when faced with the traditions, values and cultural mores of others. This may, on occasion, make us feel uncomfortable at best and, at worse, clash significantly with our own culture. Britain (and other multi-racial, multi-cultural countries) has lots of potential for cultural discomfort and culture clash. The Church in Britain lives in this context.

In scripture the Holy Spirit endorses the principle of valuing everybody across cultures. In Acts 10:1-10, Peter is sent to witness to a gentile – a man of a different culture. He felt constrained to do so, in spite of his cultural difference, because God told him to do it. What he saw and heard made him aware of God's desire to reach beyond the Jews to people of every tribe and nation. God's embrace was to bring together all in Christ. Peter's response to this observation was, "I now realise how true it is that God does not show favouritism but accepts men from every nation who fear him and do what is right" (Acts 10: 34-35).

Reality and response

At a fundamental level, we all need to be up front, and this is particularly true for leaders, about the attitudes we hold as individuals. We all have prejudices: whatever culture or racial group we come from. Very often we live with those prejudices under the surface, so to speak, and never actually confront them. But they affect our behaviour and they affect our likes and dislikes. Some of those likes and dislikes are irrational, some of them may be founded on substantial past experience.

However, it is honesty which has to undergird our approach. Church leaders have to ask, "To what extent do we want to incorporate different cultures? To what extent do we want to be multi-cultural in the widest sense of the word?"

Other pertinent questions might be, "Who do we want in our church?" and "Do we want our congregation to reflect the area we live in?" If we do want our churches to reflect their communities, then these issues of race and culture need to be looked at in terms of evangelism, pastoral care, counselling, worship, youth work and every area of ministry. Who are we trying to reach? How are we trying to reach them? Are we being culturally appropriate in the evangelistic methods we are using. Do we have anyone in the church who could contribute to the outreach programme and make it more relevant and accessible to the groups we want to make contact with?

A second area of analysis is the make-up of leadership in the church. If we have people of different racial groups, where are they in the life of the church, in terms of leadership and in terms of heading-up departments in the church? If they are not in these positions, why not? Where are they?

These questions need to be evaluated honestly, and be productive of honest answers. Heartfelt repentance and prayer needs to go into this foundation. Before God, individuals need to say that they are open to, and willing for, their church to become truly multi-cultural. These are hard issues, which lots of congregations find difficult to look at. If people hold onto their prejudices and their no-go areas, certain cultural practices will never even be looked at, or incorporated.

I'd like to quote from a letter I received from a minister who was introducing me to his congregation in preparation for a speaking engagement I had at his church in south London. He said,

> We are drawn from about forty-one different nationalities and most Sundays we have about one hundred and fifty in the main worship service, depending on how people's shift work falls! We are attempting to become truly multi-cultural, valuing and respecting everyone's culture, allowing our lives to be enriched by this cultural exposure, ready for the glory of heaven where every culture will be represented. In our services, we experience quite a variety of music and worship styles over a month. We are also blessed by a lovely blend of Pentecostals, Charismatics and Evangelicals in the fellowship.

This description of a church service which is not bound by a single cultural expression is a very poignant one for me. However, in many situations, the reality is that choices about denomination and worship style weigh more heavily than the practice of unity in Christ.

Many people say, or have heard someone say, "I go to this church because I am comfortable with it." What they are saying is that it suits their cultural background. White people say to me, "I can't go to that church because it's too noisy." Black people say, "I don't want to go to that church – they're too quiet, they are not expressive or spontaneous enough." We have got to get over this: it's not about noise or quiet, it's about who we are in Jesus. Jesus wants to bring us to a place where we can live, work and worship together as his people. We tend to negate the kingdom culture in favour of our own preferences, our earthly choices. If we do not tackle this, we will always have a black church, an Asian church, an English church. And this sends a very depressing and confusing message to the world. It says, we are aiming for heaven, but we can't work these things out here on earth.

I believe we need to have God's culture first. Although we might feel that we don't like that noise, or that style of worship, we can still say, "These people are my brothers and sisters because we are worshipping one God." I have to learn to live with my brothers and sisters here on earth, because I will live with them in heaven. Often, theological differences have added to cultural differences, to reinforce divisions.

However, as Christians we need to come to a place where we can celebrate diversity in the kingdom. We need to be able to say that it's wonderful that we are all uniquely different, and know that there is unity in the cross. There is a meeting point where we all come together, in our theology and our expressions of worship, and that is at the feet of Jesus.

It's alright to say, "*that* style is not really my style." But it's great if, when we go to church, we are open to the Holy Spirit and can truly worship. On the day of Pentecost, many culture groups came to Jerusalem to worship, and many cultures went back to their own community to carry on worshipping. There were various types of expression in worship, and when they went back to their home countries, their different forms of worship were stronger (Acts 2: 5-12).

In terms of answering some of the questions that were being raised in my mind with regard to my congregation in south London, I concluded that it would mean that our worship style should vary, that our preaching style should vary, and that we should take on board the challenge of building a church that would reflect all cultures.

On one occasion, I took the church choir to an Anglican church in Dover. However, I forgot to brief the choir on the kind of church to which we were going. I forgot to point out that this was not a Pentecostal church; that these people wouldn't speak in tongues; that some Anglicans are charismatic, but some are not, so take it easy! When we got there we went into a prayer meeting, and straight away there was a blast of tongues as all the choir members began to pray.

I opened my eyes and saw the local church officials and members raise their eyebrows in astonishment. After the prayer meeting had finished, I said what I should have said earlier, that for some of the members of this church, tongues were new, so we should meet them half-way. Culture clashes are real. People can feel intimidated and alienated, and really not know what is going on. The more we interact with people, the more we learn and understand about people. Cross-cultural fellowship holds the key to learning from each other.

In those early days of my ministry, I encouraged different groups from the church, like the choir, to go to Baptist churches or Anglican churches, to give both them and others a feel for other ways of worshipping, and to learn that the prayer book is good and healthy. God hears it! Over a period of years this approach did indeed teach these members of my congregation how to conduct themselves in other denominations, and they thoroughly enjoyed themselves. I also invited groups like Operation Mobilisation and Youth With A Mission to the church to develop a greater appreciation of the diversity of God's people working for the kingdom.

Crossing cultural lines

Crossing cultural lines first and foremost requires self-awareness. The starting point is individuals looking at themselves, recognising the culture that they come from and their own 'differentness'. For many people this is a difficult thing to do because you may be a person of the majority: you consider everyone else to be 'different' and you think of yourself as 'normal'. Very often it is not until you are in a foreign country that you realise what it might be like to be 'different' from the majority! With this comes an awareness of your cultural make-up.

Some people in this country question the need for black professional support groups, or memberships which are specific to certain cultures and races. Yet ex-patriate groups are found in other countries, as well as British schools, British libraries and the like. They are there to help people affirm their culture, remember where they have come from, and help them to deal with being a minority in a foreign land.

Recognising your differentness means realising that it is not superior or inferior to anyone else's. This is step two. If your cultural differentness is not superior or inferior, then neither is anyone else's. We can begin to level up the cultural differences. With this comes the knowledge that what I have as an individual is as valuable as that which others have as individuals. This is a God-perspective on humanity, isn't it?

The relationship between evangelism and colonialism in history, and the 'missionary mentality' that was, sadly, the Christian inheritance in the nineteenth and some of the twentieth century, is all too well known. It is amply illustrated in a statement by a white Christian minister, who said, "Yes, I believe the African is my brother, but he will always be my junior brother." The sense was that the African will never be an equal brother, and unfortunately that attitude pervaded the church and society.

After recognising where *you* are, there is a need to understand that it is not possible to value others equally if we can't let go of our stereotypes. Sometimes when we see a person, stereotypical judgements just click-in automatically. If we can let go of them, we are better able to make the right approaches to people of other culture groups. We need to be able to say, I am not looking at you with preconceived ideas, but rather, I am allowing *you* to influence my thinking about you, firstly, as an individual, and secondly, as someone who has things in common with others of your cultural background.

Lastly, we need to learn from the people that we want to reach. After my visit to Ghana, I realised that my congregation in London was not just made up of Africans *per se*, but of a variety of cultural and ethnic groups from Africa. It is important to get close to the people in your congregation. We can't rely on the media for this information. There has to be a lot of socialising and interaction.

On a fundamental level, if as church leaders we want to lead and pastor in spiritual and practical ways, and if we are dealing with a racial mix in our congregations, we need to understand the differences between cultures. This kind of appreciation will facilitate every area of our ministry.

Two key areas that illustrate the relevance of cultural awareness to the life of the Church, are the areas of counselling and evangelism. Learning from every racial grouping enables us to know how to access cultural groups. When Jesus spoke to the Samaritan woman at the well (John 4: 6-26), he knew exactly what the issues were for that woman. He knew what she was talking about, and he knew what to say. The 'opener', in evangelism, in relationships, and in every area of ministry, is often something that is relevant to the individual. Cultural awareness can give us the button to press to make that connection.

Understanding different family units and roles is also vital to counselling and pastoral work. In some black African communities, parents choose the marriage partner for their child. This is not the case in West Indian families (although there may be some objections about which island the intended partner comes from, or his or her family comes from). In certain African communities though, an individual cannot simply make their own choice.

This was an issue I had to deal with and learn to work sensitively with as I observed how important parents are in the choosing of a marriage partner. That choice has very little to do with whether the partner is a Christian or not. It is more to do with which part of the country their family comes from, their culture and background. I didn't know this when I started work in my first church, and I had to learn it, put it into practice and tread carefully and diplomatically in these areas. I could have marched in and said, "The marriage partner is a Christian, let them get on with it," and ridden rough-shod over parents and the family group.

I had to learn to honour such traditions and the people that live by them. The Bible and the word of God does, of course, have the higher hand when we are dealing with different customs, because biblical principles and convictions take precedence. I found that people did honour my biblical perspective, my faith and my Christian principles in these delicate situations.

Training for relevance and relationship

I am still amazed today by the number of people training for the ministry who have not got friends from different cultures. Many of them are going into inner city areas, with no cultural sensitivity whatsoever! It is evident that if we are embarking on any ministry that involves different cultures, we have to get closer to these groups than it is possible to do from the pulpit.

It is important that we prepare our future pastors and leaders to be more and more aware of the global implications of modern life. If we are going to stay socially relevant in the twenty-first century, we need to have relationships on a grass roots basis among different racial groups. In the past, the presentation of Christianity has been made on our own (British) terms. We haven't sought to learn or to meet other people half-way in order to speak the gospel into their culture. Sadly, there is still a good deal of ignorance in the church regarding other people groups living in Britain, particularly the African-Caribbean community. Many church leaders only know what the media feeds them. The only meaningful way we will reach other people is to get into relationship with them, making friendships, sharing meals together, and not just for six months, but over many years.

In terms of our training and theological schools (some of which I have been involved with), we must give our future leaders more than a single teaching module on 'cross-cultural orientation'. Many students are destined for inner-city churches and situations, but their head knowledge needs to be replaced by practical hands-on experience. For example, I would suggest that it would be appropriate to spend two years, of a three-year course, in a minority context, living with a minority family, working in a minority church.

As well as the theory, the practical education gives an understanding of the people they will eventually work with, pray for, lead and counsel. It doesn't matter what context you end up in; it doesn't matter which cultures you meet; people respect and appreciate someone who is effective, who knows the situation they are going into, and who is filled with God's spirit.

Some years ago I spoke at a theological college to a mixed group of students. During my talk I referred to the importance of cultural exposure. At the end of the class one student approached me and queried whether the content of the session was relevant to her, given that she lived and worked in a "middle class white suburb". Immediately I thought, "How short-sighted!" My verbal response, however, was to point her to scripture, where we find that the disciples are suddenly led out of their familiar setting, into the multi-cultural contexts of 'Jerusalem, Judea, Samaria and the ends of the earth' (Acts 1:8).

College deans and principals need to ask themselves, "How do we help church leaders to understand these issues and get involved in them in a practical way as they train?" We need to make greater strides towards cross-cultural awareness so that we will not miss the people we are trying to reach because the building blocks for relationship are lacking. It also concerns me that so few trainees from minority groups enrol at theological colleges in this country (not to mention the disturbing rate at which the colleges are haemorrhaging these groups). I would say that one reason for this is that the colleges are not catering for such groups, nor are they effectively addressing their marketing at them.

To tackle this vacuum, missionary and training organisations need to build relationships with minority churches. What tends to happen is that the relationship begins and ends with a preaching engagement. There is no deeper commitment to a broader web of support from either party. Secondly, theological colleges need to get alongside the churches that are sending out black missionaries and workers (and there aren't many), to support and resource them, to promote missions and the choice to go into ministry.

Unity in diversity

So how do we define a multi-racial church? If the leaders are white, and eighty or ninety per cent of the church is black, is it a multi-racial church? Many would say so. If the leadership is black, and eighty or ninety per cent of the congregation is also black, it is often thought that that church is not multi-racial, but black. Is a church multi-racial because of its leadership, or because of the make-up of its congregation? Do people feel uncomfortable if they are white and see black people leading the church, and vice versa?

The words 'multi-racial' and 'multi-cultural' are often clichéd, or used flippantly. On one level, the term 'multi-racial' refers to people of different racial groups, and their mixing together in whatever context. At a deeper level though, the term 'multi-cultural' encapsulates freedom of expression and involvement. A multi-cultural church is one which incorporates diversity and equality at all levels: a church where the reality of people's lives is expressed and appreciated, where people are encouraged to teach others about their cultures, and where Christians are developed and pastored in the context of their cultural background. It is a place where different races and cultures help to form the policies and the vision, and through them the complexion of the church is shaped.

In church and theological college seminars I have led, I have put the question, "What colour was Jesus?" The reply I most frequently hear is that it doesn't matter. This is the easy way out. *It does matter.* The issue of a Caucasian, Euro-centric Jesus is a big one. There are many portraits of the Last Supper, many in West Indian homes, in which all the disciples and Jesus are white, but Judas's skin is a shade or two darker. The same group also appears in other paintings in which all the figures are black-skinned. Both of these depictions cause offence, and not necessarily when a black person views the white portrait, or when a white person views the black portrait.

The colour of Jesus does matter to people, and a white Jesus or a black Jesus can cause offence. When people today see a white Jesus they ask, "What does that mean for me? What does it mean historically, socially and in terms of my experience of life?"

As an evangelist, I need to ask myself whether a Euro-centric Jesus is the best image to portray when I am preaching. How do I differentiate this image of Jesus (or other images of Jesus in other colours), from the Jesus of the cross? Our business should be to make a bridge for people to come to Jesus, and remove the stumbling blocks that stand in the way for many. If we categorically say that Jesus was white, then this is a stumbling block, and it does not affirm people as we should be seeking to do as we take the gospel message out.

When we make any presentation of our faith we should be aware of Jesus as a whole package. History has portrayed a white Jesus and a white Christianity. Some elements of this white Christianity have endorsed slavery, and the oppression of many nations (of course, others fought to end it). In some cases the image of Jesus has endorsed a history of oppression, suppression and barbarism. As a consequence, in the UK we are seeing a growing group of young people who are becoming disaffected. They are turning away from Christianity, and one of the lynchpins of their argument is the colour of Jesus. In order to take away that stumbling block, there is a lot of value in talking about a non-Euro-centric Jesus.

What has effectively happened is that the history of Christianity has been lost. By this I mean the fact that the first church was in Africa, that Israel is at the top of Africa and that Christianity is, in origin, a Middle Eastern religion. All this is an important emphasis for young black people. In this context, many people can better relate to Jesus

Christ, and the source of this presentation lies in the geographical and historical origins of Christianity.

I would say that it is very important how we portray Jesus *for some groups*, and that as churches, we have to be sensitive to the materials and resources used to present Jesus. If I have a blond-haired, blue-eyed Jesus in a European context, I would say there is no problem. But if I am going to Africa or the Caribbean, for example, or among minority groups in this country, I would want to portray Jesus pictorially as someone people could identify with and relate to.

In the Buddhist religion, statues of Buddha always bear the facial features of the country that they are to be sold in. This is an accepted practice, and it has arisen because as an Asian religion, which includes the Chinese, Japanese and the Indians, it is evidently thought valuable to assist these different races to identify with Buddha. Although it might sound as if man is trying to make God in his own image, there is nevertheless an element of wisdom in this: people want to identify with the thing that they are worshipping. The colour that people think of when they are presented with Jesus does matter. If we are to have a white Jesus in our evangelistic and teaching resources, then we need to seriously look at having a black Jesus (with kink hair), an Asian Jesus and a Chinese Jesus, too. Dealing with these issues helps us to examine ourselves as servants of Jesus, in terms of our ability to affirm people, and testify to a God who is not exclusive.

The Church has begun to rise to the challenge of true 'multi-culturalism' because it is so central to world evangelism and the demonstration of kingdom life. Jesus said, 'By this all men will know that you are my disciples, if you love one another' (John 13: 34-35). The words of Jesus challenge the church as a community of people to face cultural and racial diversity, demonstrated in unity, mutual respect and the ability to work together: a witness to the world of what it means to be a Christian and a disciple of Jesus.

Six

RESTORATION

Although as a church we felt sorrowful about the collapse
of the planted congregation, there were many encouraging
signs of growth in the 'sending' church. We were seeing
God do many wonderful things and people developing in
their faith, and yet I was aware that there needed to be
change in the organisational structure and in the way the
church was run. If we were to move more effectively into
social action I knew that there would have to be some
alteration to the way the church was resourced financially
and how it was structured in terms of leadership.

While I was watching the literal expansion of our
church as the building work for the new centre began, I
became more and more frustrated about the limitations
placed upon me with regard to fulfilling our long-term
strategy. I believed that I was getting nearer and nearer the
ceiling of what I was able to achieve.

The Executive committee, or leadership, of the
denomination, while seeming to have a sympathetic ear,
were unable or unwilling to accept that my church, because
of its size and fast rate of growth, was a special case, and
needed to be treated differently to other congregations. I
wasn't asking for favours, but for the leeway to develop
further the vision that I believed God had given us. I
wanted to be assured that as my congregation grew, I
would have significant financial independence to be able to
fulfil the vision. For example, if I needed money to employ
staff or to fund a project, I would not have the
denomination restricting me by requiring a large
proportion of the church's income.

Financial intractability became, to my mind, a real
hindrance to growth, and made me realise that I was
pulling in the opposite direction to the Executive
leadership. Besides this, I knew that after the new church

building was completed we were going to need a youth
pastor and a centre manager as a minimum, and this would
be a significant annual outlay. At this time our yearly
'income' as a church was around £100,000, and I asked the
Executive if we could retain £35,000 of this to go some
way to meeting these new costs. The church itself would
raise the rest over and above its normal giving to pay for
the extra staff. This proposal was rejected.

I felt it was not possible to run a church the size of
ours and maximise its potential with only two full-time
staff (myself and another pastor). Yet the call for more
financial resources for more personnel brought with it the
charge (in some quarters), that I was power-hungry and
was planning to install a personal secretary in my office!
The culture at that time in that denomination was that the
pastor did everything. I, on the other hand, was saying that
I needed to give myself to prayer, teaching and the spiritual
development of the congregation. Others should come in
with ministries like administration, to make the various
parts of the body function properly.

When I realised that there would be no shift in
opinion at Executive level, I put forward a proposal to
pioneer a church in East London, for which I would take
no salary. I suggested that when the church grew, ten per
cent of our finances would be submitted to the national
organisation, and the rest the church would keep to
administer itself. I was quite willing to do this, but equally
adamant that the church should not labour under the
existing financial arrangements and be penalised for
growth. Again the answer was no.

I was looking for a way to stay within the
organisation, but each path was blocked. I began to think
that I would have to resign from the ministry and resume

my itinerant role of previous years. It was tough to contemplate leaving the job, but harder to think of leaving the denomination itself. I knew I needed to step back and give myself time to reflect.

A planned two-week visit to Canada gave me that opportunity. It was while I was there, during many sleepless nights, that I recognised that the time had come for me to resign. I loved the denomination, it was an organisation that I had felt loyal and committed to, and which had blessed and encouraged me for many years, before, as well as during, my time as pastor. It was the denomination that I had been baptised in, where I had many friends and a valued church family. I had poured myself into it in full-time ministry.

Yet I knew that to stay would do me no good, and that God didn't call me to fight a denomination and those that he had set in charge over me. The only fighting I wanted to do was with the Devil in prayer.

Louise and I prayed together a great deal, and I eventually composed my resignation letter. Before posting it, I spoke to one of my colleagues to explain to him my decision. Sadly, from this point on, it felt like the gates of hell had been opened. My whole life, ministry and character came under the microscope. I was accused of being a dictator, of acting as if the church were 'mine'. In all the years I have been in ministry, then and since, I have never heard such negativity as was contained in the response to my resignation.

I asked myself, "Are these the same people I have been working with for the last few years? Is this the same organisation I have toiled in?"

Painful parting

During this time I bumped into Lynn Green, the then European Director of Youth With A Mission, and he asked me how I was. I replied, "I feel a bit like Elijah." From this brief exchange, Lynn invited me to spend a few hours with him to talk. His advice to me was to seek reconciliation and restoration, and that if all the doors were closed to me, to leave. So I wrote another letter saying that I was willing to talk about staying on. I was then asked to meet with the Executive of the denomination. From my side of the fence, I was hoping to address the bad feeling which had arisen and the pain which I was feeling at having been accused of being a poor leader. I also wanted to know if there was any possibility of me returning to ministry with the denomination in some other capacity or in another setting.

When I went to meet the Executive committee, the first question I was asked was, "Why do you want to come back?" Here was I, seeking to rebuild what had broken down, but made to feel from the start like a desperate, condemned man. There was no open-mindedness towards the possibility of a new beginning.

There followed a grilling about my style of leadership. I was told that it was thought by many that I took unilateral decisions. I told them that as far as I knew, I had taken one unilateral decision, and one only. That was at the time when we were waiting for Local Authority funding to be approved for our building project, and many of the people on the building committee which I chaired did not want to wait any longer, but go ahead and build what we could with the money we had. I believed that the funding was secure and that we should wait for the full amount we had been promised. When the money came through shortly afterwards, and we were able to build a much bigger centre, as originally planned, I felt justified in this decision. I told the Executive that I was glad to be guilty of that decision, because the church now had a much better building than we would otherwise have had.

I was also told that my team of co-leaders had said that as a leader I was "dictatorial". I didn't know that these people felt this way. My co-leaders were people I loved and respected, and I had total confidence in them to run the church when I was away travelling to speaking engagements. It was an extremely painful experience to hear this from an intimidating panel of twelve people.

The journey home to London was the longest journey I have ever taken. I didn't really know where I was, or what I was doing. By the time I reached London I was very angry and upset. Two days later I made the final decision to leave – leave my ministry in the church and the denomination itself.

Time out

Louise and I naturally had to leave the manse where we had been living, but felt that we ought to stay in south London (we had been living in Streatham for some time). A member of the congregation offered us accommodation in her home, and that was a wonderful provision from God. We stayed there for eight months. It seemed that I was starting life all over again. I could liken my feelings at this time to those of a man who has lost everything in a house fire: a house that I had built myself, containing much-loved possessions, was gone, and everything in it was charred and burnt. I found it hard to lift my mind above the things that had been said at the Executive committee meeting, and to stop turning over and over the attacks on my character and leadership.

I did feel bitterness and I cried out to the Lord that I didn't want this to be happening to me. But I knew that my ministry hadn't started in that church nor would it finish there. I was simply going through, travailing through, this time. I wasn't sure what I would do next. I had thoughts of starting a church, and the vision that God had given me some time earlier, for Ascension Trust, was beginning to fill my head, but ultimately I knew that I needed ministry and healing myself.

The period from January to April 1993 was a very distressing time of turmoil; spiritually, physically and emotionally. I had an engagement to speak at Spring Harvest, and I didn't really want to go, but fortunately I procrastinated so much that Easter came around before I knew it and it would have been unprofessional and irresponsible to back out. My subject for the session was, ironically, Elijah. I spoke from the heart!

At Spring Harvest I discussed several options for my future with many people I knew and respected. One of those I met was Roger Forster, leader of Ichthus Christian Fellowship in London. During the week the Lord laid before me several roads, and various key leaders of UK churches asked if I would consider working with them. Although this was encouraging, I knew I needed to hear from God. I was still reconciling myself to the fact that I was no longer part of the church I had been baptised in and had so many fond memories of.

Shortly after Spring Harvest, Louise and I went to a conference in Tulsa, Oklahoma, to spend time with friends there who would pray with us about our future. We started to feel that there were enough churches in the country without starting another one, and that what we really needed was to be part of a family of believers in an established church. After four days the Lord quite clearly spoke to us and said that we should become part of Ichthus Christian Fellowship.

When I returned home I had a frank and open discussion with Roger Forster, and within three months of that meeting, I was leading an Ichthus congregation in Crystal Palace, south London. There were several important things that I knew were right about this move, particularly as I began to see God's healing for me through Ichthus following the difficult times at my previous church.

It was vital for me to be part of a church community, and in Ichthus I had the assurance that I was among people who loved and valued me. They received me so wholeheartedly that it was like coming home to a family. I knew I was among leaders who had a heart to see the world evangelised. I also saw in Ichthus a tremendous purposefulness about the need for local churches to grow and develop into evangelism and social action. This was music to my ears! It was great to know that the things that were on my heart were shared by others.

Another thing that became clear to me in terms of my healing, was that although I thought I was in need of pastoring myself, the Lord gently rebuked me and showed me that in taking on the role of pastor, I was called to stand up and bring healing to my church. It was through praying with people and encouraging people that I found strength and healing myself. I was doing what I enjoyed doing – seeing people nurtured and pastored – and yet at the same I was being ministered to myself, not just by the leadership in Ichthus, but by simply doing my job and seeing people come through into a better relationship with the Lord.

Forgiveness and healing

It took the best part of three years to get over the issues surrounding my resignation. I still bear the scars but the pain has gone. I was eventually able to see that the Lord is able to do new things, and that there is freedom and release in him. As humans we can struggle with pain and forgiveness, but I believe that if I had not let go of the past there would have been a major stumbling block in the way of my ministry.

When we face painful situations we need to lay hold of Christ's example of forgiveness. I had to pray and fast and ask the Lord to help me forgive, and not to harbour bitterness: to help me to love and help me to pray. In the first few years after my resignation, I prayed a great deal for my old church. I had to; it was part of the process of saying to God, "Don't let me get bitter, don't let me want to see evil rather than good for this church, because it's your church, not mine. It's your kingdom."

I did not want to harbour divisiveness towards God's kingdom. I wanted to see my former church prosper because it was God's church. What we need to understand as Christians is that the accuser, the Devil, is constantly seeking to bring division. We have got to have the grace of Jesus, the grace that enabled him to say on the cross, 'Father, forgive them, for they know not what they do' (Luke 23:34).

We have to say, like Stephen, 'Father, lay this charge not against them' (Acts 7:60). That is what we believe. Even in disappointment and rejection we have got to find the answer in God's word and live it out.

The gospel challenges anger with peace. It challenges hate with love. Looking back now, I thank God that I went through that process, because the experience has made me a far better servant of God today than I otherwise would have been. I would not want to go through it again, but it had a profound impact on me. It anchored me, matured me, and made me more able to help other ministers.

What about the issue of perseverance? What do you do when frustration sets in? Even God votes with his feet sometimes! The Bible says that 'God will not always strive with man' (Genesis 6:3; Psalms 103:9). I would say that when all doors are closed, we have to look to the Lord to find another way. I think it was absolutely right for me to leave the denomination, but I would have liked to have left in another way. I think this is because endings are tremendously important. I did not have the opportunity to express my thanks to my church family, or to hear them say "Goodbye". When something like that happens, and there is no closure, it is not good. It can give rise to a great deal of confusion. Indeed, ten years on, I still get asked when I'm coming back to that church!

Despite all the pain, it is important that we do things properly when we face difficulties in our church situations. If two people can't agree, then they sit down and discuss the fact that they can't work together, but whatever happens, always send someone out with a blessing, just as Abraham sent Lot out (Genesis 13:8-9).

Perhaps one of the biggest challenges for the Church in this area is to make sure that relationships are ended in a righteous way, saying to one another, "Thank you for your service, may the Lord bless you and be with you." You must not get to the point where you cannot move forward. Bitterness is disabling. When you stay in an unhappy situation, you get bitter. God does not want that and it is not good for you.

It was amazing that the Lord gave me a new family in Ichthus, but there were also people from other denominations who, although they did not necessarily know what I had been through, said that they wanted to support and encourage me. They were interested in my marriage and financial situation and, in their concern for me, these people really became a source of inspiration. It was as if the Lord opened a way for me to see the wider body of fellowship and ministry in him.

Restoring confidence

I took confidence from the fact that my giftings and abilities were well complemented by the leadership team at Ichthus; that I was surrounded by people of conviction and boldness – they were not 'yes men'. Yet I do remember that for several years I was more cautious about decision making than I had been before, and that as well as 'checking' myself, I found that Louise readily acted as a 'check', asking me if I was sure about plans for this or for that in the church.

I was greatly encouraged by the response of many in my new congregation. They had only been told a little about the situation I had come from, but they were quick to say that they believed that I was the right man for their church at the right time. They said that they were glad to receive me. There were many needy and broken people there. They had had two pastors in two years prior to my arrival, and there was a lot for me to deal with. Yet I was affirmed by these men and women, and told that I was dealing with deep-rooted problems with wisdom and skill, and with a pastor's heart.

To a large extent this period was about me rediscovering myself, and that affirmation largely came from the leadership of this small congregation and also from the central leadership team in Ichthus. Some people wondered why I was not taking on a larger role, in the central leadership team. I felt strongly that I should prove myself in the local church before accepting the invitation to join a team that had responsibility for Ichthus churches London-wide.

Seven

ASCENSION TRUST

At the time of my resignation from the pastorship in early 1994, amid all the disappointments and questions, God began to push before me an awareness that a high percentage of my ministry so far had been to white churches and white audiences in the UK. As I took time to reflect on this, I began to see in sharp focus the absence of black evangelists and black youth workers, the absence of young black people starting in theological colleges. God was challenging me to develop a ministry and organisation that was about the training and inspiration of others. It was also clear that I should not do this just in England, but around the world.

The first aim of Ascension Trust, which I founded out of this awareness, is to move and motivate the African and Caribbean communities that I have been (primarily but not exclusively) called to work with, into mission. We want to identify people with a call upon their lives, to train and develop them to go on and do something for the kingdom.

The historical geography of black peoples came into sharper focus for me at this time, in the particular shape of the 'Atlantic triangle'. This phrase refers to the historical movement of people from Africa to the Americas, and the exchange of slaves for materials to be sent to Europe. God began to show me that this took place, as we know, out of greed and for all the wrong reasons. Yet, as God spoke to the brothers of Joseph in the Old Testament, and said that what they had meant for evil, God meant for good (Genesis 45:5-7), so God said to me that my vision should be to use these trade and slave routes to get black Christians strategically placed around the world. The triangle would be in motion again, but this time with the power of the gospel, with forgiveness, and with the desire to motivate the Church.

Many times I have heard people talk about the 'Atlantic triangle' with negativity, and rightly so because many horrific things happened, but to me God was saying, "Here are my purposes for that history." My vision was for black people to go back to the West Indies for strategic reasons, to take their skills and theology, their expertise in teaching and evangelism, and complement the work that is already going on there.

Black culture and its view of mission

There has been a very low level of recruitment, training and targeting of black people to work on mission overseas. Historically, this has been the case primarily because mission organisations have been staffed by white people, and these organisations, together with the UK church in general, have thought of black people as a people in need of missionaries, not as a people who could be missionaries themselves. Publicity material has always depicted the white missionary going to the black people.

However, black people have been involved in mission work from as early as the eighteenth century, and there is a particularly strong tradition of black Americans going to the Caribbean and Africa, and Caribbeans going to Africa. Yet in Britain, the picture has been sadly characterised by stereotyping and a patronising attitude on the part of the mission organisations.

It is still the case that there is no clear strategy among mainstream para-church organisations to recruit black people to mission. It is also a concern that there is no meaningful relationship between these bodies and the black community, and that there is no investment for the training and development of black people in mission. I think that the potential in the black community for mission workers has now been recognised but this has not yet evolved into strategies for involving black people over the longer term. There are pockets of good things happening, but no large-scale drive to net the vast amount of black people who want to serve in this role.

Historically, and to their detriment, black churches have had a short-term vision, rather than a long-term one. It is important to understand the differing economic dynamics that have defined the response to mission in the black and white Christian communities. It has not been part of the black church culture to support people who want to go to the mission field. There have been pockets of mission activity from some of the black churches, but there has been no concerted effort by the majority. Evidently, a person will be disadvantaged if he or she is ready to serve the Lord but does not have the spiritual and financial backing of their church.

In the white church community, by contrast, the Church has been effective in backing individuals who have a heart for mission, and those people are often encouraged to go to theological college. Alternatively, in a white church context, a young person might serve the Lord abroad in a 'gap' year before university, and their home church would offer them financial sponsorship to do so. There are only small instances of this approach to mission work in the black church community in the UK.

For many black churches the priority has been the running of the church and doing things locally, rather than funding someone to go overseas. Secondly, it was often the case in the 1960s and 1970s that black pastors were not working full-time for the church, but held down a secular job as well. For many churches, paying someone to do the

Lord's work was not something that their thinking or theology allowed. The legacy of this situation has been the belief that church finances are to be used for the upkeep of the building, minibus or Sunday School fund, but not actually as an investment in people.

So it has largely been the short-sightedness of black church leaders that has contributed to the situation we have today. Also, because many black people have viewed their life in Britain as a temporary one, and felt that they had enough trouble holding down a job and paying the mortgage, their 'vision' has been only for mission work "back home", rather than anywhere else in the world. This was an accepted attitude. Sometimes black people would go on a so-called "mission trip" to the West Indies, and do some preaching while they were there, but they would also use the time, in part, to attend a funeral or build a house.

I must emphasise that there are people with a heart and a passion for mission, but they have taken up this role at their own expense and without the blessing of their church. I recall that one lady said to me that she had had a burden for Africa for years, but was discouraged by her pastor, who reminded her that she was a woman, had no financial support, and had no experience of preaching. I know of situations where young black men and women with a heart to serve God in mission work, face isolation from their church instead of support because, sadly, it is often thought that acting on one's own initiative is being disobedient to the authority of the church.

Preparing the ground for mission

When I visit a church under the auspices of Ascension Trust, I often find that church leaders think that there is a hidden agenda: why have I really come to their church? It's one thing to say to leaders, "We want to train your people to bring souls into your congregation." It's quite another to say, "We want to train your people so that they can work effectively for the kingdom of God, regardless of the local church or denomination." It is uncommon for people to look at another church or community and say, "Hey, you're struggling over there, let me help you." So as I set up Ascension Trust, partnered by Len Davis who had left his home in Dorset to work with me, the challenge was to confront the "You work in your vineyard, and I'll work in mine" mentality of the black church culture.

You can't run before you can walk, so my task was to build trust and relationships, in order to help people to see that we wanted to serve the body of Christ in all its breadth and fullness. Time is one of the greatest ways of securing credibility, and after about four years of this work, we began to be invited to speak at major conferences and doors began to open.

We are contacted by people who want training because they have got a heart to share their faith within the local community, but feel ill-equipped for the task. We also see individuals who head-up evangelism departments in their church and who want to get training themselves before they train others.

Denominations also invite us to train their churches in evangelism and mission, to help them formulate a strategy and policy to motivate and excite their people for evangelism at home and missions abroad. This has come about through the targeting of black churches, going to their conferences and meeting leaders. It's not about being a preacher on the platform, but about building relationships with those churches and their leaders.

Our training programme looks at the subject of the gospel and asks, "What is the gospel?" By this we mean, "Who is it for? Is it a Eurocentric gospel? Does it speak to the black man and his life?" We believe that there is a need to unpack the gospel so that it can be approached from all cultures – so that it transcends culture – and so that as Christians we are equipped to communicate that fact.

Other subjects we cover include Culture, Identity, and Creative Evangelism. We look at ways of motivating the Church in evangelism; working with children; developing a multi-racial church; and issues of community evangelism with a strong social emphasis. At the end of the training course, we find that people are full of ideas to take back to their churches. We spend one Saturday working with a church in a very cosmopolitan area of London such as Brixton, and we challenge our students to present the gospel to the different cultures they find there.

The realisation that there is a need to communicate with a variety of people groups draws attention to things that some folks have not given thought to before. Our trainees can go from the classroom to the community, to the Church, and then on to missions in this country or abroad. Over the last ten years we have trained more than four thousand people, and worked with about one hundred churches across the country. We have taken about two hundred and fifty people on missions.

We now work not only with black churches but with some of the leading theological colleges. My concern to be involved with training colleges is twofold: firstly, to challenge the content of the curriculum and, secondly, to challenge the accessibility of the course. Does the course only deal with European church fathers? The prospectus may need to be broadened. Can the timetable be

rearranged so that some courses operate in the evenings in
order to enable more people to go through the system
while they are still in their jobs? For the same reason we
ask if the fees can be rescheduled to provide a greater
degree of flexibility. Together with this there needs to be
much more marketing among the black community of the
training that such colleges offer.

Using life skills for mission

In the past, black churches have believed that there is only
one ministry – the pastorate. Of course, there are many
other ministries, and a great need for people to use their
skills and expertise in the fields they have trained and
worked in. One of the concepts behind Ascension Trust is
a flexible attitude to mission. Many people find that
although they are eager to go on mission, they are limited
practically by their job, mortgage or family commitments.

We have realised that with the level of demands on
many people in today's society, it is short-term mission
which best fits with the lifestyle of most folk. The training
for mission at Ascension Trust is done in such a way as to
fit in with people who are in full-time work and, to this
end, it is often undertaken over three or more weekends.

Many people say to us that they don't really feel a
call to move to another country and take up residence
there. We say to them that they don't have to go abroad
for five years, they could join a mission for fourteen days!
It will not cost several thousand pounds, but a much
smaller figure that will cover flight, accommodation and
food. Other people say that they want to give two weeks a
year to mission, and have the remaining weeks of their
holiday entitlement for family time. We believe that it is

out of this kind of beginning that people will one day say that they are ready to go overseas for a year or two years to serve the Lord.

We take builders around the world to join and oversee building projects. Trainers, lecturers and business managers have also come into Ascension Trust. People with administrative skills can come along and be the administrator for a mission. They don't need to preach or teach, but they can help to organise events so that the mission is socially, practically and spiritually relevant.

It is part of the ethos of Ascension Trust that the missionary call is not just for a special person, but for the whole Church. What we say to people is, "You too could reach out to others as a missionary." It may be that you work as a truck driver, so why not drive the minibus for the mission team? While you are doing that you could share your testimony as others in the team share the gospel of Jesus.

One lady who worked with us on a mission in Ghana, was a doctor who had worked in the Far East and had recently returned to work in the UK. While we were in Accra, capital city of Ghana, we visited a man in hospital and, because of her training, this lady was able to note some of the shortages in equipment and medication at the hospital. With the help and support of friends back home, she was able to return a year later with much needed anaesthetic, not to mention four hundred pairs of glasses and enough money for the man to finish his treatment.

Another man, a friend of mine, worked as the European director of a well-known blue-chip company. He was able to pay for his flight to Ghana out of his air miles and during the mission he led seminars on business and management, in such subjects as how to set up a business;

business concepts; marketing; and global trends. That was his mission! He wanted to be practical in his faith by sharing his skills and knowledge.

A while ago we took some young people to the former East Germany to work with a church there. The cost was about £300 for ten days, including the accommodation, the flight and the food. This is a lot to most people, but we reminded parents that some of us would spend a lot of money on the pair of trainers our teenager longs for, yet we hesitate to invest in something which will have a lasting impact on their lives. A mission like this will truly be an investment in their character and their spiritual life.

For all the young people that went on this particular mission, it was the first time they had done anything like it. For some it was their first time out of the country. For others it was a shock to be part of a new culture, and to go to a church that wasn't Pentecostal. I watched them discovering these challenges, and seeing them come alive as they found things in themselves that they hadn't realised were there.

We also take groups to cities in this country, like Birmingham and Manchester. We aim to give leadership responsibilities to those in the fourteen to nineteen age bracket. They lead open-air meetings, drama, sharing times. One young man said to me, "Before I came on this mission I was a thirty-five per cent Christian. Now God has me under construction."

What happens is that young people are challenged about their faith. They don't need to wait until they are middle-aged! We believe that leadership issues and responsibilities in the Church are good for young people. Leadership should be a part of youth because it speaks about commitment, vision, purpose, conviction, and about people taking their place in society. Each year we have more people willing to go on mission with the Trust. We don't belong to their churches, but they can go back into their own local contexts and share what they have learnt. Ascension Trust really is having an impact!

Ghana

Our intention is to bring about movement within the 'Atlantic triangle', not only getting people moving across the ocean, but getting Africans to move across Africa, in terms of church planting, evangelism and social action. To do that we feel very strongly that we need a base in Africa.

As I have described in an earlier chapter, my interest in Ghana began seventeen years ago, when as a young pastor I first came to the country and experienced not only the poverty of the people, but also their zeal to achieve. It was from this point that my heart softened towards Ghana.

So when, with Ascension Trust, I began to think about acting on my concern for that country, I felt that Ghana should be the model for the Trust's work around the world in years to come. The struggles and difficulties of the lives of Ghanaians, together with the struggles of the Trust in becoming operational in Africa, were to be an important staging post pointing the way forward.

The year 2000 saw Ascension Trust purchasing a plot of land in Accra, the capital, in partnership with another organisation with a similar vision for an holistic gospel. We are now developing a centre there that will house facilities for doctors and dentists from the UK, who will treat patients during their 'mission' visits. There will also be facilities for a midwife and a nurse, and small operations will be performed on site. The centre will also provide accommodation for people who go to Ghana from this country on mission. Our long-term vision is that at this centre we will be able to train people from other African nations and use this base in Ghana as a bridgehead to move into other parts of Africa.

It is planned that this building will also be a place for the training of young people. Ghana is currently experiencing a tremendous move of people from rural areas into the cities and they come with no skills for getting jobs. We want to train these youngsters in practical skills and provide access to schools for them. Outside Accra, in Konongo, where we currently are based while we await the completion of our building, we have been involved in raising money to build classrooms for schools.

Church partners

We always work in partnership with local churches. As well as being the best way to operate in terms of utilising people who are 'on the ground', we have also found that we can draw together many of the small initiatives that are going on, which by themselves are very fragmented. There is something of an individualistic attitude among the churches in Ghana, and by and large, churches are failing to look at the issues and join forces in order to be more effective.

When we are preparing to lead a group of people in mission to Ghana, we will look for churches that have a heart for social action, and we will talk through with them how we can help and complement what they are doing. It falls short by a long way of the sort of impact that can be had when churches work together in unity, but as we are often working in short-term situations, it is vital that we present to churches the potential of cooperation and the limits of parochialism.

From our point of view, as we are often working at such a distance from Accra, it is very important for us that we are in partnership and dialogue with established and credible churches. We have sat down with church leaders to explain these issues and try to help them expand their vision for their city.

Street crime

'And you will be my witnesses in Jerusalem, and in all Judea and Samaria, and to the ends of the earth' (Acts 1:8). With the worldview that Jesus commanded, Ascension Trust has its eyes firmly fixed on 'Jerusalem', our home country, and its many needs. We want to stay in touch with what is happening here economically, racially, socially and spiritually. We maintain a national focus as much as we do an international one.

As a member of society, I know I need to stay in touch with what is happening on my doorstep. I know that as I read the papers and watch the news, meet and talk to people, go to the market, or ride on the bus, that without wishing to stereotype or be patronising, I see certain lifestyles and hear certain arguments. I am aware that there are bad things going on right under my nose.

I first became involved in what has become known as the 'Guns on our streets' project during a visit to Jamaica in 2001. It was not a scheduled trip; I was leading mission teams in St Vincent and Guyana, but the father of one of the co-leaders died, and I detoured to Jamaica with her to visit her family. While I was there I felt that I should go to Kingston because, by coincidence, it was twenty-five years since I had made my only other trip to Jamaica, and I really wanted to see how the church was responding to the pressures of Kingston's status as the home of reggae. I knew that Trench Town, in particular, was living up to the name created for it by Bob Marley in his song "Trench Town Rock".

I wanted to learn from the way the church in Kingston was addressing the issue of gun crime on its streets, and take home some ideas that could be applied to the rising tide of similar problems at home. I met with Bobby Wilmott, the pastor of Covenant Community Church in Trench Town.

The first thing that hit my heart was a project the church had undertaken to convert some disused communal shower and toilet facilities into a school. This had been an uphill struggle for the church as the funds to achieve it had been hard to obtain, but an amazing work was being done among young children.

Those who attended the school were children who came from very disadvantaged homes, probably way below the poverty line. Their parents were likely to be into hustling, prostitution or gun crime. Then Pastor Wilmott drove me around the locality in his car, and I was impressed by the way rough-looking young men who, to my mind, looked like the last sort of people to give a pastor the time of day, were greeting him and being respectful. Clearly Bobby Wilmott was a man of stature and integrity in the community, and he had a relationship with these disaffected young men and was able to engage with them.

Later I met another minister who had opened a factory in Trench Town for the purpose of creating wealth in that community and giving work to people who could not otherwise get employment because of their postcode. His factory was broken into many times but he kept going. That was the Church in action in Kingston.

I invited Bobby Wilmott and another pastor, Bruce Fletcher, to come to London to share what they had learnt over the years living and working in such a community. The official statistics are that in one year alone, five hundred people are shot dead in Kingston, and I wanted others to be able to hear these people talk about how they carry out the work of God in this context.

Presenting the awful truth

Initially, the 'Guns on our streets' tour was catering only for pastors, and we travelled around churches with the aim of helping British church leaders to understand the seriousness of gun crime in our communities. I wanted it to be a catalyst to stir-up the Church and provoke it into formulating strategies to work in partnership with communities to help stop these violent crimes.

The first prayer meeting was held in South Street Baptist Church in Greenwich. We shared the platform with Ian Crichlow, a member of Trident police squad, and he led a video presentation used by the police which opens with a true-life recording of a woman's 999 call. She screams, "They've shot him! They've shot him! They've shot him ten times!" This woman's boyfriend had been shot before her very eyes inside their home, and the gunman had calmly walked away.

In another scene, the camera showed a car with three bullet holes in it, then panned across to show a hat discarded on the ground and leather boots pulled off, presumably so that the victim could run faster.

The last image was of a young man, shot dead, his face and shirt singed with gunpowder because he had been shot at such close range. The eye witnesses reported the fact that the three young gunmen had walked away laughing. As you can imagine, this had a massive impact on the people at that prayer meeting.

We took the 'Guns on our streets' tour to Brixton, Harlesden, Tottenham and Mile End. People were amazed that the Church was involved in this kind of event. Of course they shouldn't be, because the Church should have the heart and compassion of Jesus to help the weak and the poor and those who feel hopeless. Out of the tour came a challenge to churches to do something for their communities; to act with a perspective on their boroughs, their cities and our nation.

Ascension Trust was then asked to chair some meetings in Manchester, to help the various community agencies – family, police, Local Authority and educational authorities – to work together.

We have found time and time again that these four areas are relevant to much of what has gone on in the lives of the young men who are causing such grief in their cities and towns. Young men who have never known a relationship with a father; young men who have dropped out of the education system; young men whose values seem to have been dented; young men who will be incarcerated or die because of their lifestyle.

The erosion of a value system

Our first meeting was in Brixton. During the day we had meetings with different leaders in the community; councillors; ministers; police; and in the evening we held an open meeting. The vast majority of our audience that evening were elderly African and Caribbean ladies and gentlemen. They were very ready to discuss the issues, and in particular to make the connection between the problems of society today and what they described as the culture clash that took place in the Sixties when they, two generations ago, had arrived in Britain from the West Indies and Africa.

I heard these men and women acknowledge the fact that their children had not been established in a value system, and typically had had their own children very young. They knew, as a consequence, that their grandchildren did not have the respect or regard for family life that they would have liked. They didn't have what they called "manners". Whereas they had been brought up to live within what was often a tight budget, and to take pride in the one-roomed houses they lived in, they could see that later generations wanted money in their pockets so that they could spend it fast.

I felt that these ladies and gentlemen were truly angry, and were practically ready to march on the streets to proclaim their indignation about the erosion of their traditions and culture.

You could argue, rightly so, that these changes are common to all cultures over the last forty years or so. However, these senior citizens were remembering a culture, a foundation to family life, which meant that the whole community could say to each other, "We are extended family." The African-Caribbean way of bringing up children was that people looked out for each other's children. Indeed, in Africa, there is a saying, "It takes a whole village to raise a child." When they came to this country, this structure was sharply undermined.

In Sixties Britain, and of course in an urban setting, it was impossible to live the way they had done back home, where they knew all the local children and where even a stranger could chastise and discipline a child who misbehaved. It was not a licence to abuse, it was quite acceptable. One woman said that back home her community had been so close that if she saw a young person up to no good, she could say, "You are Mr Jones's boy. What are you doing?"

By contrast, in British cities they saw things happening around them that they did not like but, not knowing the youngsters or their families, they felt powerless to do anything about it. This was the start of the erosion of their cultural system for those people I listened to at the Brixton meeting.

I must emphasise that the vast majority of black men and women are upstanding people, working and contributing to the fabric of society. However, as with British society as a whole, we are seeing a breaking down of values. One instance of this is the increase in teenage pregnancy. Young women are choosing to have children when they are children themselves, and to opt out of the education system. It seems that there is something about motherhood that replaces for them a lost sense of value in themselves.

We have to realise that in many cases, these are people starved of love. Often, when you probe deeper, you find that behind the scenes there is a parent missing from their own childhood.

I must also commend the many single parents who do a fantastic job, often working in a professional capacity at the same time. But we must all acknowledge that it is a fact that when a child comes into the world and there is only one parent around to bring the child up, it is an extra challenge for that individual man or woman, and a big challenge for the child itself.

Material values

To understand the best we can the culture behind gun crime, we need to understand the value system among the young men involved in it. Primarily, there is a lack of respect for human life, and with this, a materialism which both drives them to crime and also provides the rationale for their contempt of other human beings. It is a code of ethics which places more value in designer trainers or a silk shirt than in human life.

Imagine, for example, someone with these values at a party. Another partygoer treads on his toe, or makes a comment about his hairstyle, and straight away he is looking to inflict some sort of injury on that person. He does not recognise the value of life, only the fact that he has been 'dissed', or disrespected.

Secondly, there is no work ethic among this group of men. They do not say, "Let me work and save, and buy when I can afford it." These people want to get their money now and spend it now.

If a man finds he is respected because of the gold chain around his neck or the car he drives, and there has been a lack of respect for him as an individual as he has grown up, he comes to believe that his value lies solely in what he can acquire. A gun is just another item in this list of valued accessories. Stealing, or selling drugs, is often the only way to get the right things for the right image.

Values to benefit our world

As we followed up the Brixton meeting and looked at the reasons behind these problems, we felt strongly that there were five key values that we as Christians wanted to promote in the face of gun crime on our streets.

> The sacredness and sanctity of human life.
> Valuing and honouring the community.
> Being a person of integrity: it's not about what you wear but about the person you are. Martin Luther King summed this up by saying, "It's not about the colour of my skin, but the content of my character."
> Taking personal responsibility.
> The growth and development of the individual to their full potential. All of us have skills and attributes which we could contribute positively to our communities and our world. We all need encouragement to recognise these things and express them.

As I have already said, the police were part of our prayer and discussion meetings from the start. The police recognise that there is a major problem in our cities, and they also recognise that the Church can play a significant part in the reduction of gun crime. Often, many of the boys involved in such street crime have connections to a church; they may have been brought up in a church, or a mother or father may be a churchgoer, a girlfriend, a sister or brother. The police want to look at ways to persuade these young men that their way of life is bad for them and for their communities. However, the role of the police is largely preventative, to stop these awful crimes happening in the first place.

What we have done so far is to raise the profile of the issue and it is now receiving more serious debate, and not just talk, but action. Indicative of this is the level of media interest that has been received. Within a week of our first meeting in Greenwich we were interviewed by Christian television channels, BBC Radio 4, BBC Radio Five Live, the World Service, and various newspapers. We know that this is a very big issue, and we are aware that we need to think carefully about how we resource it and take it forward. We knew at the outset that the foundations of the work must be shaped by prayer. Now as we look ahead to the next stage, we feel strongly that we must get to know the young people caught up in serious street crime and personally engage with them and their lifestyles.

At the same time as I look to the future of Ascension Trust, I reflect that my own past is bound up with the problems and issues that have been aired during the 'Guns on our streets' project so far. I too was part of that history of cultures clashing, families breaking up, kids testing out their own rules and rights on the streets.

The voices that I hear as I travel around the country – voices which deplore the collapse of African and Caribbean traditions, or voices which are full of nostalgia for lost values – could be one and the same with the voice I can still hear in my head, "Hey, kid, ya got any mangoes, boy?"

The childhood memory of that old man's voice encapsulates for me the journey from Antigua to Islington, its poignancy guaranteed by the sudden transition from the familiar home to the strange city. Likewise I could express the 'before' and 'after' of my turning to Christ as another pair of extremes: the life I led as a delinquent teenager and the life I led after Jesus Christ became Lord of my life.

Yet as I see it these extreme points along a scale only provide simple snapshots, not the big picture. Though I believe that God's forgiveness is whole and complete, able to separate us from our sins as far as the east is from the west (Psalms 103:12), in the big picture, I know that I live day to day right in the forgiveness and mercy that I find at the cross of Jesus. As Christians, we have not just one moment of turning to Christ, but many, in the knowledge that God's mercy is full and flowing every day. God's works are progressive and we are on a journey with him and towards him. Let us praise God that he does a multitude of 'new things' for us all (Isaiah 43:19).